HEALTHCARE, INSURANCE, AND YOU

THE SAVVY CONSUMER'S GUIDE

Lisa Zamosky

apress®

Healthcare, Insurance, and You: The Savvy Consumer's Guide

Copyright © 2013 by Lisa Zamosky

This work is subject to copyright. All rights are reserved by the Publisher, whether the whole or part of the material is concerned, specifically the rights of translation, reprinting, reuse of illustrations, recitation, broadcasting, reproduction on microfilms or in any other physical way, and transmission or information storage and retrieval, electronic adaptation, computer software, or by similar or dissimilar methodology now known or hereafter developed. Exempted from this legal reservation are brief excerpts in connection with reviews or scholarly analysis or material supplied specifically for the purpose of being entered and executed on a computer system, for exclusive use by the purchaser of the work. Duplication of this publication or parts thereof is permitted only under the provisions of the Copyright Law of the Publisher's location, in its current version, and permission for use must always be obtained from Springer. Permissions for use may be obtained through RightsLink at the Copyright Clearance Center. Violations are liable to prosecution under the respective Copyright Law.

ISBN-13 (pbk): 978-1-4302-4953-5

ISBN-13 (electronic): 978-1-4302-4954-2

Trademarked names, logos, and images may appear in this book. Rather than use a trademark symbol with every occurrence of a trademarked name, logo, or image we use the names, logos, and images only in an editorial fashion and to the benefit of the trademark owner, with no intention of infringement of the trademark.

The use in this publication of trade names, trademarks, service marks, and similar terms, even if they are not identified as such, is not to be taken as an expression of opinion as to whether or not they are subject to proprietary rights.

While the advice and information in this book are believed to be true and accurate at the date of publication, neither the authors nor the editors nor the publisher can accept any legal responsibility for any errors or omissions that may be made. The publisher makes no warranty, express or implied, with respect to the material contained herein.

President and Publisher: Paul Manning
Acquisitions Editor: Jeff Olson
Editorial Board: Steve Anglin, Mark Beckner, Ewan Buckingham, Gary Cornell,
    Louise Corrigan, Morgan Ertel, Jonathan Gennick, Jonathan Hassell,
    Robert Hutchinson, Michelle Lowman, James Markham, Matthew Moodie,
    Jeff Olson, Jeffrey Pepper, Douglas Pundick, Ben Renow-Clarke,
    Dominic Shakeshaft, Gwenan Spearing, Matt Wade, Tom Welsh
Coordinating Editor: Rita Fernando
Copy Editor: Terry Kornak
Compositor: SPi Global
Indexer: SPi Global
Cover Designer: Anna Ishchenko

Distributed to the book trade worldwide by Springer Science+Business Media New York, 233 Spring Street, 6th Floor, New York, NY 10013. Phone 1-800-SPRINGER, fax (201) 348-4505, e-mail orders-ny@springer-sbm.com, or visit www.springeronline.com. Apress Media, LLC is a California LLC and the sole member (owner) is Springer Science + Business Media Finance Inc (SSBM Finance Inc). SSBM Finance Inc is a Delaware corporation.

For information on translations, please e-mail rights@apress.com, or visit www.apress.com.

Apress and friends of ED books may be purchased in bulk for academic, corporate, or promotional use. eBook versions and licenses are also available for most titles. For more information, reference our Special Bulk Sales–eBook Licensing web page at www.apress.com/bulk-sales.

Any source code or other supplementary materials referenced by the author in this text is available to readers at www.apress.com. For detailed information about how to locate your book's source code, go to www.apress.com/source-code/.

Apress Business: The Unbiased Source of Business Information

Apress business books provide essential information and practical advice, each written for practitioners by recognized experts. Busy managers and professionals in all areas of the business world—and at all levels of technical sophistication—look to our books for the actionable ideas and tools they need to solve problems, update and enhance their professional skills, make their work lives easier, and capitalize on opportunity.

Whatever the topic on the business spectrum—entrepreneurship, finance, sales, marketing, management, regulation, information technology, among others—Apress has been praised for providing the objective information and unbiased advice you need to excel in your daily work life. Our authors have no axes to grind; they understand they have one job only—to deliver up-to-date, accurate information simply, concisely, and with deep insight that addresses the real needs of our readers.

It is increasingly hard to find information—whether in the news media, on the Internet, and now all too often in books—that is even-handed and has your best interests at heart. We therefore hope that you enjoy this book, which has been carefully crafted to meet our standards of quality and unbiased coverage.

We are always interested in your feedback or ideas for new titles. Perhaps you'd even like to write a book yourself. Whatever the case, reach out to us at editorial@apress.com and an editor will respond swiftly. Incidentally, at the back of this book, you will find a list of useful related titles. Please visit us at www.apress.com to sign up for newsletters and discounts on future purchases.

The Apress Business Team

This book is dedicated to the idea that getting and paying for healthcare should be something that every American understands how to do.

Contents

About the Author..ix
Acknowledgments xi
Introduction xiii

Chapter 1: A New Healthcare System............................ 1
Chapter 2: Buying Health Insurance on Your Own 17
Chapter 3: Paying for Health Insurance........................... 37
Chapter 4: Health Insurance at Work 51
Chapter 5: Cutting Medical Costs................................ 75
Chapter 6: Buying Prescription Drugs 89
Chapter 7: You Against the Healthcare System 101
Chapter 8: Medicare... 117
Chapter 9: Taking Charge of Your Healthcare Future 135
Appendix: Consumer Assistance Programs and State
Departments of Insurance 151

Index 165

About the Author

Lisa Zamosky is a healthcare journalist who has been writing about how to access and pay for healthcare for more than 10 years. She is a consumer health columnist for the *Los Angeles Times*, a health reform expert for WebMD, and a correspondent for two news services of the California Healthcare Foundation. Her work has also been published in Reuters, USA Today, MSNBC, Health.com, *Chicago Tribune*, and *The Baltimore Sun*, among other publications. Zamosky previously spent a decade working in the healthcare industry, during which time she developed benefit plans for Fortune 500 companies and state governments and oversaw provider network operations for several states throughout the Northeast for one of the country's largest health insurance companies.

Acknowledgments

I'd like to thank the following people for encouraging me to undertake and complete this book. To start, it was Apress' Jeff Olson, who suggested I take on this project and gave me the opportunity to do so. He, along with Rita Fernando and her team of editors, provided me with much-needed support along the way.

A note of great appreciation goes out to colleagues who read parts of this manuscript at various stages and provided valuable feedback: Valarie Basheda, Douglas Dalrymple, Ross Blair, Linda Blumberg, and Salynn Boyles.

Special thanks to Sande Drew, who connected me with needed resources, provided ideas and inspiration, and who through this process has been a constant reminder that there was a light at the end of the tunnel.

I'm always grateful to my dear neighbor and friend Adam Reingold, who probably forgets it was he who got me started as a professional writer, and whose encouragement throughout the years has helped to keep me moving toward my goals.

Much love and appreciation to my family—especially my parents Alan and Lila Steinhart—who take such great interest and pride in my accomplishments.

I thank my son Jacob for putting up with my face nearly always being glued to a computer screen during this past year, but continuing to love me anyway. Most of all, my husband Alan deserves credit and my endless gratitude for his help in producing this book and all that I create. Without his love and support—not to mention his willingness to edit everything I write—so little of what I do would be possible.

Introduction

The tone of the letter was desperate. The writer, a man in his mid-40s, just learned that his wife had stomach cancer. The situation was grim, and not only because his wife, a 45-year-old woman and the mother of four young children, was very sick.

The couple had health insurance, the man said in his letter, but they were being denied the coverage for a surgery the doctors said was necessary for his wife to survive. He was desperate. What was he supposed to do? How would he get his wife the care she needed if the insurance they bought to protect them in just these circumstances wouldn't pay for her medical care?

We can treat and manage illnesses today that years ago would have killed us. But without the ability to pay for care, and a traveler's guide of sorts to help us navigate the fragmented American healthcare system, all the medical advances can't help us. In the United States of America, healthcare and money are inextricably linked.

As a healthcare columnist writing for the *Los Angeles Times* and WebMD, I regularly receive many letters like this man's from people who are struggling to understand the best way to access healthcare and utilize their own health insurance policies. As in the case of the man and his wife, sometimes that struggle—and whether people are able to push their way through successfully—can mean the difference between life and death.

Others I hear from are in less dire straits, but struggling nonetheless with issues that can have a dramatic impact on their health and finances.

Many people try in vain to get a copy of their medical records, for instance, and face a doctor or hospital that refuses to cooperate with their request.

Others are treated at hospitals contracted with their insurance company, only later to receive an enormous bill from an out-of-network doctor who claims to have cared for them during their hospital stay.

People also write to me because they are confused about their Medicare options or how to choose the right health plan among a host of choices being offered by their employer at open enrollment time.

I talk to people all the time who say they need help cutting through the red tape that comes with paying for medical care, understanding the fine print of insurance, and knowing where to turn for help when things go wrong.

And, during the past several years, questions and confusion about the Patient Protection and Affordable Care Act—the health reform law often referred to as Obamacare—have been plentiful.

That's why I wrote this book.

Getting and paying for healthcare for so many people in this country feels like a game they're forced to play without being given access to the rule book. But our health and our financial security are no game, and they're no laughing matter. Understanding how the system operates, how to get the care you need, and knowing what your insurance policy will or won't pay for are critical to both your physical and financial health.

About This Book

This book is about demystifying the system and arming yourself with the knowledge needed to take charge.

Healthcare, Insurance, and You simplifies the many confusing details about the new healthcare law and our healthcare system so you can make informed decisions and protect yourself and your family.

This book has been written as a guide that explains the main challenges you're likely to face when trying to understand the impact that the Affordable Care Act will have on your health insurance benefits and how to get excellent healthcare: choosing the best insurance policy for your situation, buying prescription drugs the least expensive way, picking out the right Medicare plan, or fighting for your rights when dealing with insurers or medical providers.

Throughout the book, I include tips, resources, and strategies for navigating the healthcare system and avoiding common mistakes.

I'll highlight and explain jargon—language commonly used in the world of health insurance that only adds to the confusion most people have about their benefits and how best to use them—and what it all means.

I'll work to give you an understanding of how things operate behind the scenes, so you'll know how and where to get the care you and your family need without breaking the bank.

In the first chapters of the book, I'll explain the health reform law in plain English so you can understand (finally!) how it's likely to impact you depending on your current situation. Whether you buy health insurance on your own, get it at work, or run a small business struggling to offer health insurance to your employees, this book will help you understand your options and whether or not you're among the millions of Americans who will now qualify for free or subsidized healthcare.

Reading this book will give you answers to the following questions:

- How does the Affordable Care Act impact my own and my family's healthcare and finances?
- How can I take advantage of the new health insurance marketplaces and tax credits?
- How do I choose a health plan that best meets my medical and financial needs?
- How do I fight billing errors and denied claims, and know where to turn for help when I need it?
- How can I avoid common mistakes that can cost me big—or even put me into bankruptcy?
- How will health reform affect my business?
- Will health reform reduce my healthcare costs?

It's important to note that as this book goes to print, policy changes and political wrangling over details of the Affordable Care Act are on-going. The basics of the law as explained in these pages aren't likely to change, but for updates readers are encouraged to use Healthcare.gov as a resource for all things health reform.

You don't necessarily need to read the book all the way through. Rather, you can use it as a reference to turn to at moments when you need answers.

Armed with information about how to initiate an expedited appeal the man whose wife was diagnosed with stomach cancer was able to get the insurer to reverse its initial decision and his wife got the surgery she needed. I know of so many other situations in which applying pressure at just the right points achieved results, in some cases, as in this one, saving a person's life.

Here, I'm going to show you those leverage points to help you get the best healthcare possible. This book is ultimately about empowering you to take charge of your health and your finances.

Let's get started.

CHAPTER 1

A New Healthcare System
Things Are About to Change—Big Time!

The Patient Protection and Affordable Care Act (President Obama's health reform law) is ushering in major changes to the American healthcare system. Millions of people will gain new access to health insurance coverage and go about shopping for and buying a health plan in new ways.

Operating Below Capacity

To understand the changes coming, it's helpful to know where we are today and how that's led us down the path to health reform.

The United States stands alone when it comes to healthcare. Many of us have come to believe that we have the best system in the world. And, no doubt, the United States is home to some of the most advanced medicine the world has to offer. But we also fall short, horribly so in fact, in some key areas.

If you've been paying for health insurance for a number of years, I don't have to tell you that premiums—the monthly cost of your health plan—keep rising. Trips to the doctor's office or the hospital have gotten pricier too. And, for millions of Americans, it seems accessing health insurance benefits has

Chapter 1 | A New Healthcare System

become a complicated maze you have to wend your way through without a road map.

■ **Jargon alert** A *Premium* is the cost of a health insurance policy. Often paid on a monthly basis, these are the payments you make to keep an insurance policy in place.

What are we getting for the high price we pay?

In America, we spend more on healthcare than any other industrialized country, and we get less for our money. Here are some quick statistics[1] to put things in perspective:

- In the United States, we spend more than $8,300 per person annually. Compare that to the $5,000 the world's second and third biggest healthcare spenders, Norway and Switzerland, spend per person.

- Despite the higher price we pay, Americans actually see the doctor and are admitted to the hospital less frequently than citizens of other countries.

- Our rates of preventable death due to asthma and diabetes-related amputations, among other conditions, are the worst among 12 other industrialized nations.

What's more, a study released by the Institute of Medicine (IOM) and the National Research Council found that people in the United States younger than the age of 50 live their lives in worse health and die younger than people in 16 other wealthy countries in Western Europe, Canada, Australia, and Japan.[2]

There are a number of reasons for our poorer health. We eat more and less nutritionally, have higher rates of drug abuse and deaths from guns, wear seatbelts less often than people in other countries, and have more alcohol-related traffic accidents. Another main reason cited for our poor health has to do with our healthcare system. Unlike other countries, we have millions of people

---

[1]Commonwealth Fund: Explaining High Healthcare Spending in the United States: An International Comparison of Supply, Utilization, Prices, and Quality: www.commonwealthfund.org/~/media/Files/Publications/Issue%20Brief/2012/May/1595_Squires_explaining_high_hlt_care_spending_intl_brief.pdf
[2]Institute of Medicine: http://iom.edu/Reports/2013/US-Health-in-International-Perspective-Shorter-Lives-Poorer-Health/Report-Brief010913.aspx?page=1

without health insurance and much more limited access to primary care. And Americans, according to the IOM report, find it harder than people in other countries to get the care they need and to be able to afford it.[3]

In short, citizens of other countries are healthier, yet in some cases the price of healthcare is about half the cost of what we pay here in America.

We are the only industrialized country that doesn't guarantee healthcare and some kind of insurance coverage to our citizens.

We have been on an unsustainable path. Fewer people are being offered health insurance at work, and employers are struggling to keep up with the cost of making health benefits available to their employees.

What's more, those among us who don't get health benefits at work and buy insurance on our own are faced with a host of challenges around getting the coverage we need to help pay for medical care, including high insurance costs and fewer benefits in exchange for the high price we pay.

Health Reform Is Changing Your Healthcare

These, and other forces, led to the passage of the Patient Protection and Affordable Care Act, also known as health reform and Obamacare. Signed into law on March 23, 2010, the Affordable Care Act represents the most significant overhaul of our nation's healthcare system since the Medicare law was passed 1965.

Many people have called the law a government takeover of healthcare. It's important to understand, however, that the most fundamental aspects of our current system—that care is delivered by private doctors and hospitals, that health plans are sold by private insurance companies, and that the majority of Americans continue to get their health insurance through their employers—remain intact.

But it is true that through the new law, insurers, healthcare providers, and employers will all face new requirements in the interest of expanding health insurance coverage to millions of uninsured Americans.

No matter where you stand on health reform—whether you believe the law is in the best interests of the country or a horrible mistake—most people agree that something fundamental about our healthcare system simply must change if it's to serve the needs of all our citizens.

Healthcare costs in this country have continued to rise at rates that far outstrip our earnings, and there is considerable fear that without finding ways to curb how much we spend on healthcare in the United States, we're going to face serious trouble. Likewise, efforts to improve the quality of the care we're

---

[3] Ibid.

paying for are underway and offer some hope for improving the inadequate level of care that comes in the form of poor coordination, a lack of preventive medicine, and medical errors that result in needless deaths each year.

Insuring the Uninsured

At least one part of the solution—and a central goal of the new health reform law—includes making sure more Americans have access to health insurance. With most of the country able to gain coverage, the theory goes, those of us with health insurance will no longer pay for those without coverage who tend to get medical care through expensive emergency room visits or who fail to catch treatable illnesses early because they don't have access to preventive care. Part of the price we pay for our health insurance includes paying for the costs resulting from medical care that goes unpaid for because some people don't have coverage.

The health reform law takes aim at our country's growing number of uninsured and makes an effort to keep future healthcare spending down. It does this largely by making changes to the way insurers and healthcare providers operate and get paid.

Big Changes: More for Some than for Others

The changes on the way as a result of the law will vary, depending on who you are, whether you already have health insurance, and where you get your coverage (at work vs. on your own).

The biggest changes, at least early on, will be in store for people who have middle or low incomes. Starting in 2014, these groups will be eligible for financial help to pay for their insurance coverage.

The law will also have a huge impact on people with pre-existing medical conditions who do not have access to health insurance through work and have been unable, because of their illness, to buy a plan on the private insurance market. Again, this changes starting in 2014, when insurers will be prohibited from turning away anyone interested in buying a health plan.

I'll get into greater detail in later chapters to describe exactly how health reform will impact you given your personal situation, but for now, here's a bird's eye view of the changes on the horizon, as well as of some parts of the law that have already started to alter the way things work.

Health reform has three primary goals:[4,5]

---

[4] Kaiser Family Foundation Summary of New Health Reform Law: http://www.kff.org/healthreform/upload/8061.pdf
[5] Kaiser Family Foundation Health Reform Timeline: http://healthreform.kff.org/timeline.aspx

1. Changing to the Way Insurance Companies Do Business

Buying insurance—especially for people who don't get it at work—is often a challenge. The law puts new protections in place for consumers and eliminates some of the most common barriers people face when trying to buy health insurance.

The two biggest changes the law makes to the current system are

- It guarantees health insurance coverage to anyone who applies.
- People with health problems cannot be charged more than those who are healthy for their insurance plans.

Insurers will also be required to sell plans that include a core package of benefits. Although details of plan benefits will vary somewhat depending upon the state you live in, the following list of 10 categories of "essential health benefits" must be included in each health plan sold. These categories are:

1. Ambulatory patient services
2. Emergency services
3. Hospitalization
4. Maternity and newborn care
5. Mental health and substance use disorder services, including behavioral health treatment
6. Prescription drugs
7. Rehabilitative and habilitative services and devices, such as speech therapy, physical therapy and occupational therapy.
8. Lab tests
9. Preventive and wellness services and chronic disease management
10. Pediatric services, including oral and vision care

These and other benefits will take effect in 2014, but the insurance industry had to change some of its other practices earlier. Some consumer protections and benefits may already be available to you. More than 50 pieces of the law had gone into effect by the end of 2012. Here are a few big ones that took effect already.[6]

---

[6]Healthcare.gov

No More Lifetime Limits on Your Coverage

Before health reform, insurance companies were allowed to—and typically did—place a cap on how much money a policy would pay out for medical care before it stopped paying completely. Caps on certain procedures were common, too—say a $200,000 limit on an organ transplant, for example.

That's no longer the case. Under the law, new insurance policies (those purchased after March 23, 2010) are prohibited from applying lifetime limits.

Paying for Preventive Care

The law has removed the cost of a number of preventive services. That means that at the time you go for care, you're not on the hook for a deductible, or co-payment, or co-insurance.

Jargon Alert *Co-pay* is a fixed fee you pay at the time of a medical visit.

Co-insurance is a percentage you pay for the cost of a medical service.

Under the law, there are 16 preventive services covered for adults that are free of charge, including screenings for blood pressure and cholesterol levels, colorectal cancers, depression, type 2 diabetes, HIV, and immunizations such as an annual flu shot.[7]

Among other services covered with no cost-sharing are 22 types of preventive care specifically for women, such as mammography screenings for breast cancer, cervical cancer screenings, and regular well-woman visits.

If you have Medicare coverage, these preventive services are also available to you without your having to pay at the time of your doctor visit.

Finally, children get access to no-cost preventive care. In fact, 26 preventive services are available to children with no requirement to pay at the doctor's office. Typical childhood vaccinations, such as those to prevent measles and tetanus as well as annual flu shots, are included. Screenings for autism and for hearing and vision problems are on the list too.

You can see a full list of covered preventive services at Healthcare.gov.

---

[7] www.healthcare.gov/news/factsheets/2010/07/preventive-services-list.html

Grandfathered Health Plans

Health plans that were already in place on the day health reform became law (March 23, 2010) and haven't made major changes to their benefits or charge considerably more for things like co-pays, co-insurance, and deductibles are considered to be "grandfathered." These plans get a pass on some of the law's new requirements, and don't have to comply with some parts of the Affordable Care Act.[8]

Jargon Alert *Grandfathered health plans* are health plans that started on or before March 23, 2010 and that have kept their benefits much the same since then. These plans are exempt from complying with some parts of the Affordable Care Act.

Parts of the Law That Apply to Grandfathered Plans

Provision	Date It Goes into Effect	Does It Apply to Grandfathered Group Plans?	Does It Apply to Grandfathered Individual Market Plans?
Young adults can stay on their parents' health plans until age 26	Health plan years starting on or after September 23, 2010	YES, with one exception: Until 2014, this provision applies only if a young adult does not have another offer of job-based coverage (excluding an offer from another parent's job-based plan).	YES
Prohibition of preexisting condition exclusions for children under age 19	Health plan years starting on or after September 23, 2010	YES	NO

(continued)

---

[8]Families USA. Grandfathered Plans Under Patient Protection and Affordable Care Act: www.familiesusa.org/assets/pdfs/health-reform/Grandfathered-Plans.pdf

Provision	Date It Goes into Effect	Does It Apply to Grandfathered Group Plans?	Does It Apply to Grandfathered Individual Market Plans?
Preventive services covered with no cost-sharing	Health plan years starting on or after September 23, 2010	NO	NO
Restriction on annual limits in coverage	Health plan years starting on or after September 23, 2010	YES	NO
Prohibition of lifetime limits in coverage	Health plan years starting on or after September 23, 2010	YES	YES
Prohibition against unfair rescissions of coverage	Health plan years starting on or after September 23, 2010	YES	YES
Direct access to OB/GYNs without a referral; pediatricians can be classified as primary care providers; enrollees must have choice of primary care providers	Health plan years starting on or after September 23, 2010	NO	NO
No higher cost-sharing for out-of-network emergency services (compared to in-network); no prior authorization requirements for emergency care	Health plan years starting on or after September 23, 2010	NO	NO
Right to internal and external appeals of insurer decisions	Health plan years starting on or after September 23, 2010	NO	NO

Source: Families USA.

How can you tell if your health plan is grandfathered? There are a couple of ways to figure it out.

(A) Check your health plan's materials. Insurers are required to indicate in the benefit materials they send you each new plan year whether you're covered by a grandfathered health plan. But it can be tough to locate this information. So your best bet may be to call the plan to find out. Insurers are required to include information about whom to contact and how to get in touch with them if you have any questions or complaints.

(B) Ask your employer or your health plan's benefits administrator. If you get your health insurance at work, ask the folks who manage benefits for your company (this could be someone in the human resources or benefits department or an outside company hired to do this). Keep in mind that even if the health plan is new to you it could still be considered grandfathered if your company offered this plan before you began working there.

If you are enrolled in a grandfathered group health plan but changes made to either the benefits included in your plan or the amount you pay for coverage seem significant, you can file a complaint by contacting the U.S. Department of Labor at 1-866-444-3273 or www.dol.gov/ebsa/healthreform.[9] Want more detail? Here are the specific changes a plan can make that would disqualify it from being considered grandfathered.

Changes That Disqualify Plans from Grandfathered Status

Plan Element	Disqualifying Change*
Co-payment	The greater of an increase of more than $5 (adjusted for medical inflation since March 23, 2010) or an increase above medical inflation plus 15 percentage points.
Deductible	An increase above medical inflation (since March 23, 2010) plus 15 percentage points.
Out-of-Pocket Limit	An increase above medical inflation (since March 23, 2010) plus 15 percentage points.
Co-insurance	Any increase in the co-insurance rate after March 23, 2010.
Annual Limit	Any decrease of an annual limit that was in place on March 23, 2010 disqualifies a plan. Adoption of a new annual limit for plans that did not have one on March 23, 2010 also disqualifies a plan.
Employer Premium Contribution Rate (in group plans)	A decrease of more than 5 percentage points below the existing employer contribution rate as of March 23, 2010.
Benefits Package	The elimination of all or substantially all covered benefits to diagnose or treat a particular condition after March 23, 2010.

---

[9] http://cciio.cms.gov/resources/files/are_you_in_a_grandfathered_health_plan_04072011.pdf

New Rights for Appealing Insurance Denials

Before the Affordable Care Act became law, you may have had the right to appeal decisions made by your insurance company—say, denied authorization for treatment or refusal to pay for care you already received. However, some people did not have that right. Whether or not you did varied based on where you lived and the type of insurance you had. Under the new law, insurers must review their decision to deny paying for your care. If you are not satisfied with the outcome of that appeal, you now have the right to appeal a second time to an independent reviewer that does not work for the health plan.[10]

Children Can't Be Turned Down

As of September 23, 2010, insurers selling new policies are no longer allowed to deny any child younger than the age of 19 a health plan, even if he or she has a pre-existing medical condition.

The same benefit will be available to adults starting January 1, 2014.

Young Adults Can Stay on Their Parents' Health Plan

The law now allows adult children to remain insured by their parents' health plan up to the age of 26, even if they don't live at home or are married (but the adult child's spouse cannot be covered). However, if your parents are covered by a group plan that existed on March 23, 2010, and you have an offer of insurance through your job, you may not be able to sign on with your parents' insurance plan. That restriction will end, however, on January 1, 2014.

To date, nearly 3.4 million adult children who before the law didn't have health benefits now get health insurance this way.[11]

Drug Cost Relief for People on Medicare

If you have Medicare coverage and take a lot of medications, you likely know about the Medicare donut hole—the gap in prescription drug coverage that starts once your drug costs reach a certain limit. In 2013, you enter the donut hole once your total retail drug costs amount to $2,970. You'll remain in the

---

[10]Families USA. Your Right to Appeal: www.familiesusa.org/health-reform-central/september-23/Your-Right-to-Appeal.pdf
[11]Kaiser Family Foundation: Employer Health Benefits, 2012: http://ehbs.kff.org/pdf/2012/8345.pdf

gap and on the hook for the full cost of your medications until your drug costs amount to $4,750, at which point your plan will begin to pick up 95% of your medication costs.[12, 13]

Before health reform, anyone in the donut hole paid for the full amount of his or her medication costs, which can present a major financial hardship for many seniors and people with disabilities who rely on Medicare.

The health reform law aims to shrink the donut hole over time. In 2013, you'll receive a discount on name brand drugs of 52.5% and an 11% discount on generics. Over time, the discounts grow. By 2020, if you hit the donut hole you'll pay just 25% of the cost of both name brand and generic prescription drugs.[14]

The government estimates that in 2013, Medicare recipients who reach the prescription drug donut hole will save $766 as a result of the law. By the year 2020, the savings amount rises to $2,217.[15]

2. Making Health Insurance More Affordable

The law aims to do this in a number of ways: First, it expands the Medicaid program—health insurance for people with low income. If you are an individual who makes about $15,400 a year or less, you'll qualify for Medicaid, which will give you access to health insurance at no or very low cost.[16]

Second, people with incomes below a certain threshold may be eligible for subsidies from the federal government to help cover the cost of health insurance (more on this later). In fact, a family earning as much as $94,200 (in 2013) may qualify for some financial help to pay for a health plan.[17]

Still, for many Americans, health insurance remains an uncomfortably pricey product. I'll discuss this in greater detail in the chapters that follow.

In addition, for the first time in this country, most people will be expected to have health insurance, a requirement of the health reform law referred to as the "individual mandate."

---

[12]Allsup. Understanding Medicare Part D Plans: www.allsup.com/personal-finance/managing-healthcare-costs/maximizing-your-medicare-drug-coverage.aspx
[13]Medicare.gov: www.medicare.gov/Pubs/pdf/10050.pdf
[14]Healthcare.gov. Medicare Drug Discounts: www.healthcare.gov/law/features/65-older/drug-discounts/index.html
[15]Healthcare.gov. Medicare beneficiary savings and the Affordable Care Act: www.healthcare.gov/news/reports/affordablecareact.html
[16]Urban Institute: http://nohla.org/pdf-downloads/Urban%20Institute%20Report%20FAQ%20.pdf
[17]Kaiser Family Foundation: http://healthreform.kff.org/coverage-expansion-map.aspx

The individual mandate has been the most divisive part of the Affordable Care Act. In fact, lawsuits that made it all the way to the Supreme Court attempted to overturn the law, claiming in part that the requirement for most U.S. citizens to buy health insurance coverage was unconstitutional. The court ruled in the summer of 2012 that the law did not violate the constitution, as the lawsuits claimed. As a result, starting in 2014 you'll either have to have health insurance or pay a tax penalty for opting not to.

3. Changing the Way Healthcare Is Delivered and Paid for

Currently, healthcare spending accounts for 18% of the annual United States economy, or $2.7 trillion.[18] The Affordable Care Act includes new programs that aim to alter, the way healthcare is paid for and delivered, with the goal of reducing the amount of money we spend as a country. The hope is that broader efforts to rein in costs will eventually lower the amount each of us pays for insurance.

The law attempts to lower costs largely by changing the way doctors and hospitals are paid. Instead of fee-for-service reimbursement in which providers make more money for doing more, quality-based payments intended to encourage doctors and hospitals to deliver better-coordinated and preventative care at a lower cost will increasingly be adopted.

Rolling Out the Law

The health reform law has been taking effect in stages. Although it was passed in March, 2010, and some parts of the law have already gone into effect, health reform's most significant changes won't happen until 2014.

Here are some of the biggest changes you'll want to know about.

Pre-Existing Medical Conditions

As I mentioned earlier in this chapter, one of the most significant pieces of the health reform law is that it will soon be illegal for insurance companies to deny anyone a health plan because of his or her medical condition. That takes effect starting January 1, 2014.

Why does this matter?

---

[18] Centers for Medicare & Medicaid Services (CMS): www.cms.gov/Research-Statistics-Data-and-Systems/Statistics-Trends-and-Reports/NationalHealthExpend Data/Downloads/Proj2011PDF.pdf

If you aren't one of the 149 million Americans[19] who get their health insurance through your job or your spouse's company, and have a medical condition, you likely know that buying a health plan on your own is an exercise in futility because:

- Insurers simply won't cover you if you have a serious illness such as heart disease or type 2 diabetes.
- You may get approved for a health plan, but it excludes coverage for your preexisting medical condition—the very reason you most need health insurance in the first place.
- An insurance company agreed to sell you a health insurance policy, but because you've been sick before, or are in mid or late life (but too young to qualify for Medicare), the prices are unaffordable.

Starting January 1, 2014, the game changes for people who have gone without health insurance, not because they don't want it, but because they:

- Don't work for a company that offers insurance coverage, and they have a health condition that has prevented them from buying a policy.
- Can't afford it.

A New Way of Buying Health Insurance

Jargon Alert *Health Insurance Marketplaces* are online shopping sites where people will be able to buy a health plan.

If you buy health insurance on your own, don't have health insurance now, or work for a small business, the health reform law creates a new way for you to shop for benefits.

The law calls for the creation of Health Insurance Marketplaces. Think of Marketplaces as health insurance supermalls where you'll have the chance to shop for and compare multiple plans side by side. In addition, if it turns out you qualify for a tax credit from the federal government to help you pay for coverage, or you qualify for Medicaid, that will be made clear to you and you

---

[19]Kaiser Family Foundation Employer Health Benefits 2012: http://ehbs.kff.org/pdf/2012/8346.pdf

will have the option of having the tax credits applied directly to the price of your health plan during the buying process to lower your monthly costs.

Online health insurance Marketplaces will be available nationwide. Each state must have one, although some states will run their own market while others will be run by the federal government. That will all happen behind the scenes, though, and shouldn't be noticeable to you, the healthcare consumer.

We'll talk more about these markets in later chapters.

Rising Healthcare Costs Are Changing Your Healthcare

As I mentioned, most people in this country still get their health insurance at work and will continue to do so after the health reform law has taken full effect.

As the cost of healthcare rises, employers work to keep their expenses under control, in part by shifting more of it to their workers in the form of higher premiums, co-payments, and co-insurance. In addition, they are finding new ways to create incentives for people to get and stay healthy and to encourage them to receive care from healthcare providers that demonstrate their ability to provide high-quality care at reasonable costs.

Employers are offering high-deductible health plans to their workers at a growing rate. These plans require that you pay $1,000 or more out of your own pocket before your insurance company helps you pay for your medical care. That means it's becoming increasingly important to understand how much tests and medical procedures cost before you head to the doctor.

As the nature of health plans change, so too must our approach to accessing healthcare services. Runaway healthcare costs have inched us ever closer to an age of consumerism, when we must think about our medical care and its costs much the way we do when buying any other good or service. This marks a dramatic change in the world of healthcare, and barriers still exist when it comes to learning the true cost and the quality of the medical services we need.

Regardless, becoming savvy about the best place to get your care, how to negotiate for the best price, how to use new tools to understand in advance what your costs are likely to be and how to maximize your health benefits will become more important as time goes on.

No longer can we take a passive role in our healthcare. The future requires us all to be more knowledgeable.

Summary

The new health reform law, along with rising healthcare costs and efforts underway to gain some control over them, mean big changes are ahead.

The law will provide many new protections for healthcare consumers and offer financial help for millions of people who have struggled to afford insurance coverage.

Still, for many of us, health insurance and healthcare are likely to remain expensive. That's why becoming a savvy healthcare consumer is so important. And doing so means understanding how the Affordable Care Act, and the healthcare system as a whole, operate and the direct impact they will have on you personally.

If you're currently without health insurance or you buy your own coverage on the private market, Chapter 2 offers you a clear picture of what the health reform law has in store for you, and what the future of health insurance benefits are likely to look like for you and your family.

CHAPTER 2

Buying Health Insurance on Your Own

New Ways to Shop and Pay for Coverage

If you don't currently have health insurance or buy coverage on your own, big changes are in store for you. The Affordable Care Act brings new guarantees of health insurance coverage, as well as new protections and benefits with the plan you buy. You may also qualify for financial help to lower your insurance costs.

Insuring the Uninsured

People without access to insurance through an employer, as well as middle- and low-income Americans, stand to gain the most under the Affordable Care Act.

Today, nearly 46 million Americans live without health insurance.[1] Being uninsured has serious consequences. It can limit your ability to access needed medical care, which can threaten both your physical and financial well-being.

---

[1] Centers for Disease Control and Prevention. Health Insurance Coverage: Early Release of Estimates From the National Health Interview Survey, 2012

People without health insurance are less likely to get preventive healthcare services, such as screenings for breast and colon cancers. In many cases, the lack of access of the uninsured to preventive health services leads to hospitalization for preventable health conditions. The uninsured are also more likely to die in the hospital.[2]

Millions of people without insurance skip out on care they know they need. For example, almost 60% of those with a chronic health condition who lack benefits report not filling a prescription because of the cost.[3]

Families that go without health insurance are at greater risk of having to spend down all of their savings or go into credit-card debt to cover the cost of their care.[4] Ironically, people without health insurance also tend to pay the most for the care they do receive. Without an insurance company negotiating lower rates on their behalf, the uninsured are charged as much as four times the amount for hospital services paid by health insurers and public programs.[5]

A growing number of Americans have simply been priced out of the health insurance market. Others have been shut out of the market because a pre-existing medical condition makes them unattractive to insurers.

Maybe you're interested in retiring early—before you qualify for guaranteed health insurance coverage under the Medicare program—but have continued working because of a lack of health benefit options once you leave your job. Or perhaps you've dreamed of starting your own business but have stayed in a job with topnotch health benefits you know you'd never be able to replace if you went out on your own.

Americans have long faced barriers when it comes to gaining access to health insurance when they don't have an offer of coverage through their job. The Affordable Care Act will dramatically change the way the health insurance market functions, giving millions of Americans more health insurance options and, in some cases, greater choice about how they work and live.

In this chapter, we'll cover in greater detail three primary parts of the Affordable Care Act, and how they are likely to impact you and your family:

1. Expanding insurance coverage to millions of Americans
2. New ways to shop for health insurance policies
3. Financial help available to reduce the cost of health insurance

---

[2]Kaiser Family Foundation. The Uninsured: A Primer:
http://kaiserfamilyfoundation.files.wordpress.com/2013/01/7451-08.pdf
[3]Commonwealth Fund. The Price of Being Uninsured:
www.commonwealthfund.org/Resources/2013/The%20Price%20of%20Being%20Uninsured.aspx
[4]Kaiser Family Foundation. The Uninsured: A Primer
[5]Ibid.

A Guarantee of Coverage

Today, more than one in five people (22%) who attempt to buy a health insurance policy on the private market are denied because of their health status.[6] Sometimes the health issues are minor. Insurers may turn someone down because of a medical diagnosis, even if it was provisional and eventually changed or because symptoms reported on the application suggest a possible health problem brewing.

Jargon Alert *Private Insurance Market* is where people buy health plans on their own.

These are people like Kelly, a 42-year-old woman with diabetes. Kelly works for a small business that doesn't offer health insurance. For her, buying health insurance on the private market has been impossible.

Without insurance coverage, she has been forced to pay more than $500 per month for the insulin she needs to keep her diabetes in check. Unlike millions of other Americans, Kelly is lucky because her parents are able and willing to help her pay part of the cost of her medicine. "Without their help, I wouldn't be able to afford it," she said. "I don't know what I would do."

There are people like Kelly all over this country who have been unable to access health insurance and the physical and financial protection it offers. The healthcare overhaul will change this for them in a number of ways.

No More Denials

As I briefly discussed in Chapter 1, the Affordable Care Act expands coverage to millions of Americans who today cannot get health insurance in part by changing the rules insurance companies must follow.

Starting January 1, 2014, anyone who applies for a health insurance policy is guaranteed coverage, regardless of whether he or she has a current or past medical condition. It will no longer be legal for insurers to turn anyone down.

---

[6]HealthPocket. Health Insurance Application Rejection Rates Rising: www.healthpocket.com/healthcare-research/infostat/health-insurance-application-rejection-rates#.UZvngLVJNU8

Chapter 2 | Buying Health Insurance on Your Own

> **NEW ACA BENEFIT!**
>
> One of the most significant new features of the Affordable Care Act starts on January 1, 2014: You can no longer be denied an insurance policy because you're sick—or because you were previously treated for a medical condition or illness.

Fairer Pricing

If you have a pre-existing medical condition, you cannot be charged more for a health plan than someone who is perfectly healthy. Kelly, for example, will pay no more for her policy than someone without a history of diabetes or other illness who purchases the same plan.

And women, who have historically paid higher prices for health insurance than men (the argument goes that women use more medical services than their male counterparts), can no longer be charged more for the same health insurance policy.

There are only three circumstances under which someone can be charged a higher rate for insurance:

- **Age:** Older people will pay a higher rate for coverage than the young, but the difference in price will be capped at a ratio of 3 to 1. That means if you're 63, you will pay no more than three times what a 23-year-old pays for the same health plan. Today that ratio can be as high as 10 to 1.

- **Geography:** The cost of providing medical services is higher in some geographic locations than others. Insurers can factor these variations into their rates.

- **Tobacco use:** The federal law allows insurers to charge people who smoke one and a half times more than non-smokers. However, some states have made it illegal for insurers to do so. In addition, you won't be charged the full surcharge if you enroll in a smoking cessation program.

Jargon Alert *Health Insurance Marketplaces* (also referred to as Exchanges) are the new health insurance shopping websites being set up under the Affordable Care Act. There will be one established in each state, either by the state itself or by the federal government.

Guaranteed health insurance to anyone who applies for coverage marks a significant change from the current insurance market. Today, people without a perfect health history who don't get insurance through an employer are often denied coverage or charged so much for a health plan that coverage remains out of reach.

The law provides two main paths to health insurance for those who currently buy it on their own or who are without coverage.

Path 1: The Medicaid Expansion

Medicaid is the joint state–federal program that today provides medical benefits to roughly 60 million people across the country with low incomes.[7]

Eligibility for Medicaid varies from state to state, but today, the program primarily covers adults who have children, low-income pregnant women, children, people with disabilities, and elderly people with extensive medical needs. If you have a low income but in the past have been unable to qualify for Medicaid, you've likely been left without any other affordable health insurance options.[8]

Jargon Alert *Medicaid* is the joint federal and state–government funded health insurance program for people with limited income and assets.

New Guidelines for Medicaid Eligibility

As written, the health reform law requires that all states expand their Medicaid program starting in 2014. States that failed to do so would run the risk of losing all of the federal money they currently receive to help pay for their existing Medicaid programs.

In exchange for expanding Medicaid eligibility, however, the federal government will pay 100% of the cost for the first three years starting in 2014, then 90% from then on. Most states were expected to comply with this part of the law.

However, in the summer of 2012, the Supreme Court ruled that states now have the option to expand their programs without the threat of losing their current Medicaid funding. It's no longer a requirement of the law.

---

[7]Consumer Reports. Health Reform: Seven Things You Need to Know Now: www.consumerreports.org/health/resources/pdf/ncqa/The_Affordable_Care_Act-You_and_Your_Family.pdf
[8]Kaiser Family Foundation. Medicaid Expansion Under The Affordable Care Act, JAMA, March 27, 2013: http://jama.jamanetwork.com/article.aspx?articleid=1672246

Why This Matters

One half of all Americans without health insurance have incomes that fall below the new earning limits to qualify for Medicaid (roughly $15,800 in 2013).

If all states had expanded their program as the law initially intended, it's expected that enrollment in Medicaid would increase by nearly 13.1 million people nationwide by 2016.[9]

However, a number of states have declined to broaden eligibility for their Medicaid programs that would include more people, while others are still on the fence. Failure to expand Medicaid coverage will leave millions of people uncovered.

It's been projected that as many as 6.4 million people with incomes below the poverty level (in 2013, $11,490 per year for an individual; $23,500 annually for a family of four) and who would otherwise be eligible for Medicaid under the new guidelines set by the Affordable Care Act, live in states not expanding their programs.[10] That means some of our poorest citizens are likely to be left without access to health insurance.

Are You Eligible for Medicaid?

There are two factors that determine if you're eligible for Medicaid under the Affordable Care Act starting January 1, 2014:

1. Whether or not your state participates in the Medicaid expansion
2. Your income

Is Your State Participating?

As of July 15, 2013, 24 states had decided to expand their Medicaid programs, 21 had declined to expand, and 6 states were still debating the issue. There's no deadline for states to decide how they wish to proceed; they can make a decision at any time to expand their Medicaid program.[11]

---

[9] Kaiser Family Foundation. The Cost of Not Expanding Medicaid: http://kaiserfamily foundation.files.wordpress.com/2013/07/8457-the-cost-of-not-expanding-medicaid3.pdf
[10] Ibid.
[11] Ibid.

Healthcare, Insurance, and You

State Decisions to Expand Medicaid, July 2013

Not Moving Forward	Debate Ongoing	Moving Forward
Alabama	Indiana	Arkansas
Alaska	Michigan	Arizona
Florida	New Hampshire	California
Georgia	Ohio	Colorado
Idaho	Pennsylvania	Connecticut
Kansas	Tennessee	Delaware
Louisiana		District of Columbia
Maine		Hawaii
Mississippi		Illinois
Missouri		Iowa
Montana		Kentucky
Nebraska		Maryland
North Carolina		Massachusetts
Oklahoma		Minnesota
South Carolina		Nevada
South Dakota		New Jersey
Texas		New Mexico
Utah		New York
Virginia		North Dakota
Wisconsin		Oregon
Wyoming		Rhode Island
Vermont		
Washington		
West Virginia		

Source: Kaiser Family Foundation.

If you live in a state that has yet to decide whether it will make Medicaid available to more people, you can continue to check on its status at Medicaid.gov.

Do You Qualify?

If you are a legal resident and a single person earning about $15,856 or less annually, or a family of four earning $32,500 or less each year, you may qualify for Medicaid (again, assuming you live in a state that has chosen to expand its eligibility requirements).

The way the law is written, Medicaid was expected to cover people who earned an income that is slightly higher than poverty level. As I'll discuss in greater detail in the next section, people with incomes as high as four times poverty level—$45,960 for an individual and families of four earning up to $94,200—are eligible for subsidies when they buy insurance through the new state marketplaces. In states not expanding Medicaid, those with annual incomes between poverty level ($11,490) and 1.38 times that ($15,856) will likely qualify for subsidies if they buy insurance through the marketplaces. However, those earning incomes below poverty level may not qualify for financial assistance from the government to pay for health insurance.

Where Can You Go to Get Medicaid?

As I'll discuss in the next section, one way to sign up for Medicaid will be through new state-based health insurance marketplaces. These virtual health insurance shopping malls are set up online and will be open for business October 1, 2013. By punching in some information about yourself and your income, you'll learn whether or not Medicaid is an option for you and be given instructions about how to sign up.

There will also be personalized assistance available to help guide people through the enrollment process, as well as the option of signing up in person, if you prefer. You can find help in your state by going to Healthcare.gov. You can also find your state contact information in the Appendix.

Path 2: The Health Insurance Marketplaces

The second path to health insurance is to buy it on your own through the new health insurance marketplaces being developed in each state.

You will be able to compare health plans side by side, learn if you qualify for Medicaid or other financial help from the federal government, and ultimately buy yourself a health plan.

These online health insurance shopping sites will open for business around the country on October 1, 2013, for individuals, families, and small business owners. Policies purchased in the fall will go into effect January 1, 2014.

Here's what you need to know about shopping for health insurance through the marketplaces.

Open Enrollment

There is an initial open enrollment period that will run between October 1, 2013 and March 31, 2014. If you enroll no later than December 15, 2013, your coverage will be effective January 1, 2014.

If you enroll in January, February, or March in 2014 between the first and 15th of the month, your coverage will start the first day of the following month.

Those enrolling between the 16th and the last day of the month will have coverage that takes effect the first day of the second following month.

Date You Enroll	Date Insurance Takes Effect
October 1, 2013–December 15, 2013	January 1, 2014
January 1–15, 2014	February 1, 2014
February 1–15, 2014	March 1, 2014
March 1–15, 2014	April 1, 2014
January 16–31, 2014	March 1, 2014
February 16–28, 2014	April 1, 2014
March 16–31, 2014	May 1, 2014

In the future, the open enrollment period will run between October 15 and December 7.

If you miss out, you'll be left uninsured until the following open enrollment comes around. That means you'll likely be charged a tax penalty (see Chapter 3 about the tax implications under the law) and be at risk for high medical costs if you become sick or injured during the gap.

There will be special enrollment periods available for events that bring changes to your life and impact your insurance coverage—divorce, marriage, death of a spouse, or loss of employer-sponsored health benefits.[12] In addition, if you take a job that offers health insurance or become eligible for Medicare or Medicaid, you'll receive coverage even if it falls outside of the open enrollment period.

Standard Benefits

Insurers interested in selling health plans through the new state-based marketplaces are all required to include services that fall within 10 categories of care referred to as "essential health benefits."

---

[12] Leavitt Group. Exchanges/Health Insurance Marketplaces for Individual Coverage: Eligibility and Enrollment: www.leavitt.com/NewsAndEvents/HealthCareReform.aspx?eid= 7934301177029711182

All plans sold across the country must include the essential health benefits package. However, states have flexibility to determine the specific services included within each category. That means the details behind what's covered in the health plans sold through the health insurance marketplaces can vary from one state to another.[13]

ESSENTIAL HEALTH BENEFITS

Under the Affordable Care Act, every insurance plan sold must cover the following categories of benefits:

1. Ambulatory patient services
2. Emergency services
3. Hospitalization
4. Maternity and newborn care
5. Mental health and substance use disorder services, including behavioral health treatment
6. Prescription drugs
7. Rehab and habilitative services and devices (e.g., help with developmental issues; hearing aids and speech therapy; vocational and educational therapy, such as those needed by children with autism spectrum disorders)
8. Laboratory services
9. Preventive and wellness services and chronic disease management; this includes women's access to contraceptives, sterilization, and emergency contraceptive pills (Ella and Plan B One-Step) at no cost
10. Pediatric services, including oral and vision care

Standard Costs

There are four different types of plans that can be sold through the marketplaces. All must cover services in each of the 10 categories discussed earlier. They will differ by how much they pay, on average, toward the cost of services the health plan covers.[14]

---

[13]Families USA. Implementing Exchanges: www.familiesusa2.org/assets/pdfs/health-reform/Selecting-Plans-for-Exchanges.pdf
[14]Ibid.

The plans are referred to as "metal levels"—bronze, silver, gold, and platinum. Insurance companies participating in the marketplaces must offer a minimum of at least one silver and one gold plan and at least one plan that covers only children; however, this can vary by state. Insurers will also offer what are called catastrophic plans to people younger than the age of 30, or who cannot afford another type of health insurance.[15]

Generally, you will be required to buy at least a bronze-level plan to meet the minimum requirements for insurance under the law. (Those eligible for the catastrophic plan are exempt.)

Here's how the plans break down:

- **Bronze:** A bronze level plan covers 60% of the average enrollee's costs for covered benefits. That means your plan pays 60%, and you pay 40% in the form of deductibles, co-payments, and co-insurance.
- **Silver:** These plans cover 70% of medical costs, while you're left to pay 30%.
- **Gold:** This level plan pays for 80% coverage and you pay 20%.
- **Platinum:** 90% of costs are covered under a platinum plan, leaving you to pay the remaining 10% of costs.
- **Catastrophic plan:** Anyone younger than the age of 30 is eligible to buy a catastrophic health insurance policy. People who are exempt from the requirement to buy health insurance because they don't have an affordable coverage option or because they qualify for a hardship exemption, can also buy a catastrophic plan. The coverage with this type of plan is more limited and includes higher out-of-pocket costs when you seek medical care. However, costs are waived for preventive services (wellness visits, mammograms, colonoscopies, and the like) and three visits to a primary care doctor each year. It's important to note that individuals purchasing catastrophic plans are not eligible for premium tax credits.

Note Dental coverage is an essential health benefit for children, but not for adults. The benefit must be made available as part of a child's coverage. You will be able to buy dental plans through the health insurance marketplaces; some will be included with the health plan, others will be sold separately.

---

[15]Community Catalyst & Georgetown University Health Policy Institute. Health Insurance 101: What Are Federal Subsidies? http://101.communitycatalyst.org/aca_provisions/subsidies

Limits to Out-of-Pocket Expenses

Health plans sold through the marketplaces must cap the total amount you're required to pay in annual out-of-pocket expenses, including deductibles, co-pays, and co-insurance. The limits are the same as the out-of-pocket limits that apply to high-deductible plans used with Health Savings Accounts (HSAs)—$6,350 for a single person and $12,700 for a family (2013 numbers).[16]

Standard Application Process

There will be one standardized application to fill out when applying for health insurance coverage. Once completed, you will be able to see all of the insurance options from which you can choose. The coverage options will be based on the income you report.

Starting October 1, 2013, you can apply for a policy through your state's marketplace or by logging onto Healthcare.gov.

If you'd rather not handle this process online, you'll have the option of printing an application that you can fill out and mail in or talk with someone by phone who can walk you through the process.[17]

Summary of Benefits

To make it easier for people to compare their insurance options side-by-side, the law requires all health plans—even those offered through an employer—to provide a standard summary of benefits at the time of enrollment as well as when it comes time to renew a plan.

These are forms that show the services covered by a plan, including costs such as deductibles, co-pays, and co-insurance; the list of doctors and hospitals participating in the health plan's network; the prescription drugs covered by the plan; and a glossary of common health insurance terms, among other pieces of important information.

Also included is a tool that compares two common health scenarios—type 2 diabetes and delivering a baby—and the expected out-of-pocket costs that often accompany both.[18]

---

[16] Families USA: Implementing Exchanges: www.familiesusa2.org/assets/pdfs/health-reform/Selecting-Plans-for-Exchanges.pdf; Community Catalyst & Georgetown University Health Policy Institute. Health Insurance 101: What Are Federal Subsidies? http://101.communitycatalyst.org/aca_provisions/subsidies
[17] Center for Medicaid and Medicare Services. www.cms.gov/Newsroom/MediaRelease Database/Press-Releases/2013-Press-Releases-Items/2013-04-30.html
[18] Healthcare.gov: Summary of Benefits

Personalized Help Buying Coverage

Each state must offer personalized assistance to anyone who feels he or she needs additional help choosing a health plan.

- **Navigators and In-Person Assisters** will provide education and guidance to people enrolling in the health insurance marketplaces. They can help you fill out an application and compare available health plans to guide you through the process of selecting the best insurance option for you and your family.[19]

- **Certified Application Counselors (CACs)** are community-based organizations, such as community health centers and hospitals that will be available to help people sign up for health insurance through the marketplaces.[20]

- **Consumer Assistance Programs** will help you enroll in a health plan, understand your rights under the law, and help you file complaints and appeals if problems arise.[21]

- In addition, the law gives states the option of allowing **insurance brokers and agents** to help you enroll in a qualified health plan through your state's marketplace. You can check with your state's marketplace and/or department of insurance to learn if this is an option for you.[22] In the Appendix, I include contact information for each state where consumers can find out more information about health insurance and assistance programs.

The decision tree from the Kaiser Family Foundation (Figure 2-1) shows how people will get health insurance coverage under the law beginning in 2014.

---

[19]Healthcare.gov
[20]Georgetown University Health Policy Institute: http://ccf.georgetown.edu/all/certified-application-counselors/
[21]Healthcare.gov. Consumer Assistance Program: www.healthcare.gov/law/features/rights/consumer-assistance-program/
[22]Families USA. Brokers and Agents and Health Insurance Exchanges: www.familiesusa2.org/assets/pdfs/health-reform/Exchanges-Brokers-and-Agents.pdf

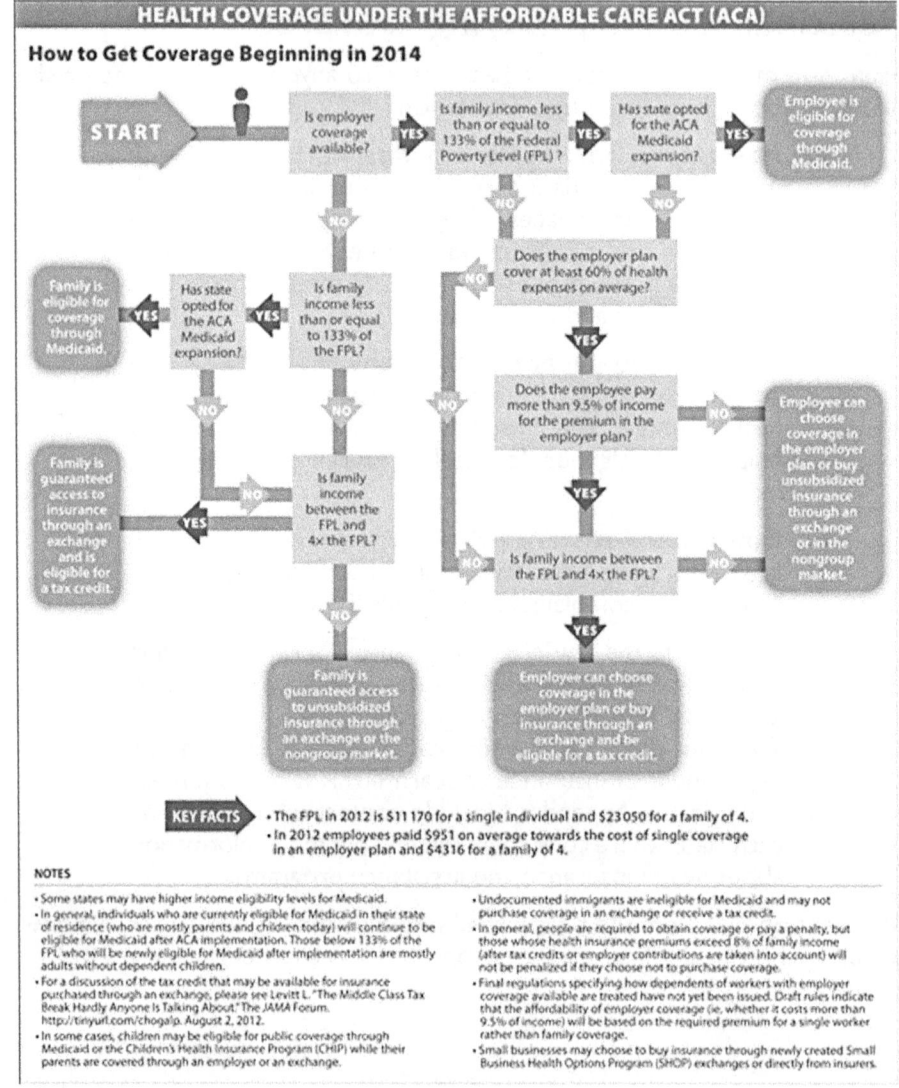

Figure 2-1. How you'll get Health insurance coverage for 2014.
Source: Kaiser Family Foundation (www.kff.org) analysis.

Choosing the Right Health Plan

The fact that benefits will be standardized into the four "metal levels," that each plan must cover the same package of benefits and must cap your total out-of-pocket spending for the year will make it much easier to compare one health plan to another. However, it's important to keep in mind that differences among the plans will still exist. You must carefully evaluate the details of each policy against your particular medical needs to make sure you're choosing the best possible plan for you and your family.

Here are a few things to watch for:

- Each plan will have a different combination of deductibles, co-pays, and co-insurance. For example, platinum-level plans will cover more of your out-of-pocket expenses, but they'll cost you more on a monthly basis. You'll get a bigger break on your monthly premium with a bronze plan, but you'll pay more upfront when you go to the doctor. All plans will cap your total annual out-of-pocket costs (again, no more than $6,350 for an individual and $12,700 for a family). However, if you rarely go to the doctor, it may be less expensive for you over the course of a year to select a plan with a lower monthly premium but that requires you to pay more each time you go for care. If you have a chronic condition and are regularly going to the doctor, however, it may be cheaper for you to pay a higher monthly premium, but lay out less money at each visit.

- Although there are no more lifetime and annual limits on how much is spent on your care, limits can be placed on the number of visits for certain types of care, such as physical therapy. If you have a particular health need, read those details carefully to make sure you're covered.

- The doctors and hospitals affiliated with the health plans will all be different. It's important to look carefully to see that your healthcare providers or professionals you wouldn't mind treating you are participating with the plan you choose.

- Drug formularies will also vary from one plan to the other. Although the law requires plans to offer one medication in every category or class, if it's not the medication you need, it may not be the right plan for you.

Do You Have to Buy Insurance?

As I mentioned in Chapter 1, for the first time in this country's history, most American citizens will be expected to have health insurance starting in 2014. Those who don't buy coverage will be assessed a tax penalty (see exceptions in the next section). This requirement of the health reform law is referred to as the "individual mandate."

To avoid the tax penalty you must have health insurance provided to you by one of the following program types:[23]

- An employer
- Coverage you buy on your own
- Medicare
- Medicaid
- Children's Health Insurance Program (CHIP)
- Veteran's Administration and/or Tricare for active duty and retired military
- Indian Health Services
- Healthcare sharing ministry

So what happens if you don't buy insurance?

The penalty starts fairly low and then rises over a period of three years. Here's how it works:

In 2014, the penalty will be 1% of your annual income or $95, whichever is greater. For a family, the penalty is $285 or 1% of household income. That means if you are single person making $35,000 per year, you will owe $350 at tax time for 2014 if you fail to sign up for an insurance policy.

That amount rises over the years. By 2016, the penalty will be 2.5% of your income or $695, whichever is greater. For a family, the maximum penalty is three times that amount, or $2,085.

You will pay a penalty when you file your income taxes each year.

This information is summarized in Table 2-1.

Table 2-1. Health Insurance Penalty Schedule

Year	Percentage of Income	Set Dollar Amount Individual/Family
2014	1%	$95/$285
2015	2%	$325/$975
2016	2.5%	$695/$2,085

---

[23]Kaiser Family Foundation. Focus on Health Reform: http://kaiserfamilyfoundation.files.wordpress.com/2011/04/8061-021.pdf; Consumer Reports. Health Reform: Seven Things You Need to Know Now: www.consumerreports.org/health/resources/pdf/ncqa/The_Affordable_Care_Act-You_and_Your_Family.pdf

Are You on the Hook?

Not everyone is required to have health insurance. There are exceptions under the law. You won't be required to have coverage or pay a penalty if:[24]

- Even the lowest cost health insurance option available to you amounts to more than 8% of your income.
- You don't file taxes because your income falls below the threshold required to do so.
- You are a member of certain religious sects or health care sharing ministries.
- You are of Native American descent and are eligible for services through an Indian health care provider (your dependents are exempt as well).
- You are incarcerated.
- You are an undocumented immigrant.
- You have less than a 3-month gap in your insurance coverage.
- Your income is low and you live in a state that is not expanding its Medicaid program.
- You are a dependent of a worker with an offer of affordable individual insurance through an employer and cannot afford insurance without federal tax credits to help lower your insurance costs.

The infographic (Figure 2-2) shows the decision tree that will help you determine whether or not you'll be required to have health insurance under the health reform law.

---

[24]Kaiser Family Foundation. Focus on Health Reform: http://kaiserfamilyfoundation.files.wordpress.com/2011/04/8061-021.pdf; Health and Human Services Final Rule. Exemptions: www.ofr.gov/OFRUpload/OFRData/2013-15530_PI.pdf

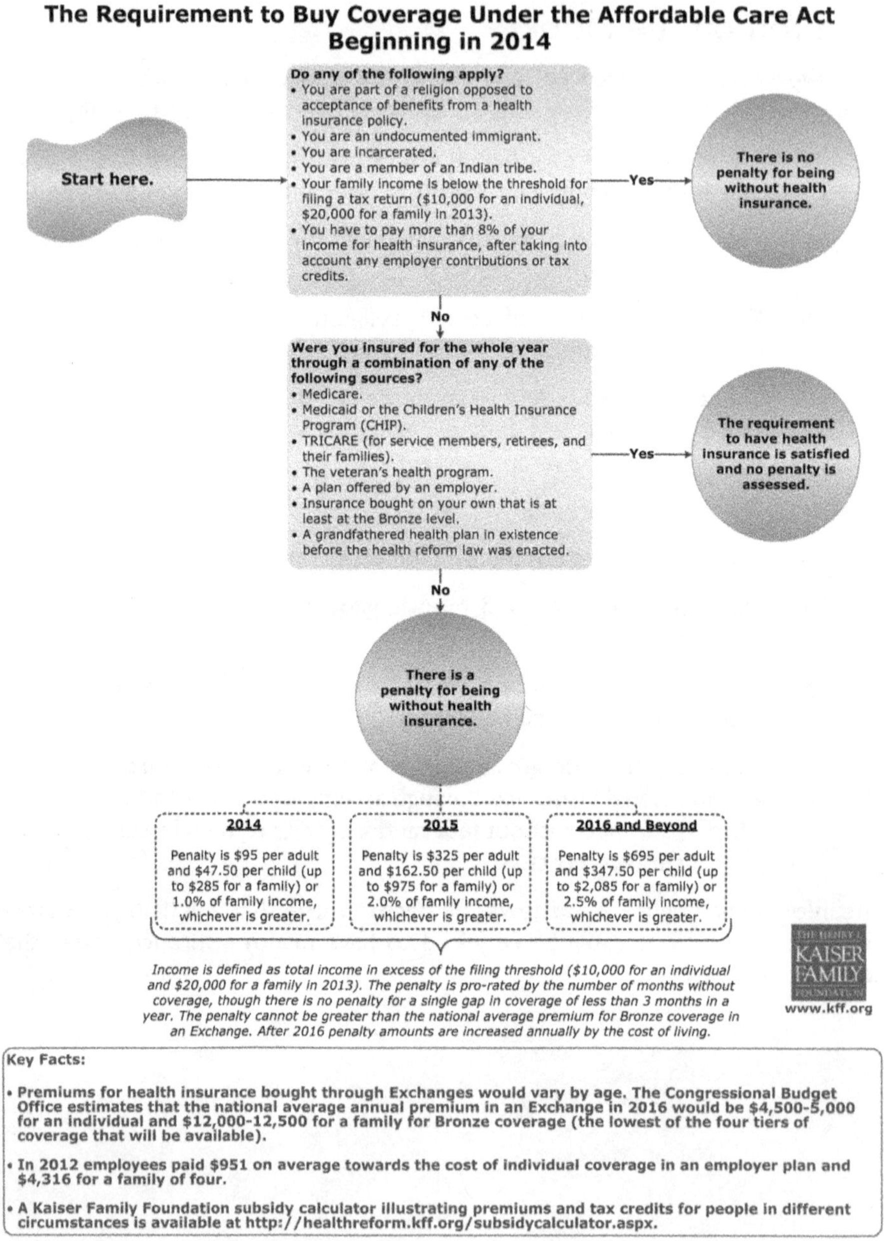

Chapter 2 | Buying Health Insurance on Your Own

The Requirement to Buy Coverage Under the Affordable Care Act Beginning in 2014

Start here.

Do any of the following apply?
- You are part of a religion opposed to acceptance of benefits from a health insurance policy.
- You are an undocumented immigrant.
- You are incarcerated.
- You are a member of an Indian tribe.
- Your family income is below the threshold for filing a tax return ($10,000 for an individual, $20,000 for a family in 2013).
- You have to pay more than 8% of your income for health insurance, after taking into account any employer contributions or tax credits.

—Yes→ **There is no penalty for being without health insurance.**

↓ No

Were you insured for the whole year through a combination of any of the following sources?
- Medicare.
- Medicaid or the Children's Health Insurance Program (CHIP).
- TRICARE (for service members, retirees, and their families).
- The veteran's health program.
- A plan offered by an employer.
- Insurance bought on your own that is at least at the Bronze level.
- A grandfathered health plan in existence before the health reform law was enacted.

—Yes→ **The requirement to have health insurance is satisfied and no penalty is assessed.**

↓ No

There is a penalty for being without health insurance.

2014
Penalty is $95 per adult and $47.50 per child (up to $285 for a family) or 1.0% of family income, whichever is greater.

2015
Penalty is $325 per adult and $162.50 per child (up to $975 for a family) or 2.0% of family income, whichever is greater.

2016 and Beyond
Penalty is $695 per adult and $347.50 per child (up to $2,085 for a family) or 2.5% of family income, whichever is greater.

Income is defined as total income in excess of the filing threshold ($10,000 for an individual and $20,000 for a family in 2013). The penalty is pro-rated by the number of months without coverage, though there is no penalty for a single gap in coverage of less than 3 months in a year. The penalty cannot be greater than the national average premium for Bronze coverage in an Exchange. After 2016 penalty amounts are increased annually by the cost of living.

THE HENRY J.
KAISER FAMILY FOUNDATION
www.kff.org

Key Facts:

- Premiums for health insurance bought through Exchanges would vary by age. The Congressional Budget Office estimates that the national average annual premium in an Exchange in 2016 would be $4,500–5,000 for an individual and $12,000–12,500 for a family for Bronze coverage (the lowest of the four tiers of coverage that will be available).

- In 2012 employees paid $951 on average towards the cost of individual coverage in an employer plan and $4,316 for a family of four.

- A Kaiser Family Foundation subsidy calculator illustrating premiums and tax credits for people in different circumstances is available at http://healthreform.kff.org/subsidycalculator.aspx.

Figure 2-2. Determining if you're required to have health Insurance in 2014.
Source: Kaiser Family Foundation.

WHY MUST EVERYONE HAVE INSURANCE?

The "individual mandate"—the requirement that most Americans have health insurance—is intended to prevent healthy people from going without coverage and simply waiting until they get sick to buy a plan now that insurers must accept all-comers.

This makes it so that the cost of medical services is shared between those who are healthy and use fewer services and people who are sick and use more. If only people with medical conditions buy coverage, the cost of health insurance would likely rise dramatically.

Jargon Alert A *Premium* is the cost of a health insurance policy. Often paid on a monthly basis, these are the payments you make to keep an insurance policy in place.

Summary

The Affordable Care Act radically changes the health insurance options available to people who purchase health insurance on their own or who are currently uninsured.

By guaranteeing insurance to all American citizens who apply for coverage and by making government funds available to lower the cost of insurance for those who qualify for subsidies or for Medicaid, millions of people are expected to gain access to coverage over the next several years.

In Chapter 3, we'll take a closer look at how the federal subsidies will impact health insurance costs.

CHAPTER 3

Paying for Health Insurance

Federal Subsidies May Lower Your Costs

Under the Affordable Care Act, the federal government will provide financial assistance to millions of middle- and low-income families. Subsidies, or tax credits, will reduce the amount many individuals and families pay for health insurance, and for some, also lower their out-of-pocket costs at the time they seek medical care.

Help Paying for Health Insurance

If there's one question people ask most frequently about new health insurance plans available under the Affordable Care Act it is: "How much will it cost me?"

There have been endless media reports warning about the potential of health insurance prices skyrocketing. And, there are reasons why prices may, in fact, increase.

First, the plans sold through the health insurance marketplaces will include more benefits than are in the plans most people buying their own coverage have today. Mental health services and maternity care, for example, must now be included as covered services in every new health plan.

Another reason for a possible hike in insurance rates is the new requirement that insurers accept everyone who applies for a health plan. That means people with higher health costs can no longer be denied insurance, and they can't be charged more for their coverage than healthy people. This may contribute to the rise in the average cost of health insurance premiums. It's possible that some people will see their insurance rates increase as the burden of cost is spread more evenly across healthy and the sick, older, and younger policy holders.

Whether or not costs rise may also depend on where you live. Some states had stricter guidelines in place for insurers before the Affordable Care Act became law. States that allowed bare-bones insurance plans to be sold, and that didn't require insurers to comply with stringent laws, may see prices rise as health plans make changes to comply with the new law. However, it should be said that health plan rates released by a handful of states by July 2013 have not shown any great spikes in prices.

However, even if there are cases where premiums do increase, most people buying insurance through the state-based online health insurance marketplaces are likely to pay less for their coverage. That's because under the new law, the federal government makes insurance premiums more affordable for low- and middle-income Americans by providing financial assistance in the form of tax credits to help pay for coverage. In fact, 26 million people—nearly 90% of those eligible to buy insurance on the new marketplaces—are expected to qualify for federal payments to help lower their health insurance costs in 2014.[1]

One study conducted by the consulting firm Milliman found that families in the state of California earning less than $60,000 a year could save as much as 84% on their premiums and 76% on the total cost of their healthcare with the help of federal subsidies.[2]

Do You Qualify for Tax Credits?

Let's get down to business. Do you and your family qualify for the tax credits that will lower the cost of health insurance for millions of Americans? If you do qualify, how do the credits work and how will you go about taking yours?

First, let's look at a few things that will determine whether or not you qualify.

---

[1] Families USA. Help Is at Hand: New Health Insurance Tax Credits for Americans: http://familiesusa2.org/assets/pdfs/premium-tax-credits/National-Report.pdf
[2] Milliman. Factors Affecting Individual Premium Rates in 2014 for California: www.healthexchange.ca.gov/Documents/Factors%20Affecting%20Individual%20Premiums%20FINAL%203-28-2013.pdf

Your Income

Your modified gross income (called MAGI) is what the marketplace will use to determine whether you are eligible for tax credits. For most taxpayers, MAGI is the same as adjusted gross income, or AGI. You can easily find your AGI on your last tax form. Here's where to look:

- If you use Form 1040 EZ – Line 4
- If you use Form 1040A – Line 22
- If you use Form 1040 – Line 37

If you're an individual with an annual income of less than roughly $46,000, or your family of four earns no more than about $94,000 a year, you meet the income requirements to qualify for a tax credit.

The amount of help you'll get depends on your family income and your family size. Lower-income families get the most help.

Take a look at Table 3-1. If your income is near the amounts shown, you may qualify for a tax credit to reduce the cost of your health insurance.

Table 3-1. Family Size and Income Qualifying for a Tax Credit

Family Size	Yearly Income
1	$45,960
2	$62,040
3	$78,120
4	$94,200
5	$110,280
6	$126,360

The law limits the amount you'll contribute to your premium for a silver-level insurance plan to a set percentage of your income. Table 3-2 shows how that breaks down.

Table 3-2. Income Table[3]

Family Size = 1

If your income is	Less than $15,280	More than $15,280 but less than $17,240	More than $17,240 but less than $22,980	More than $22,980 but less than $28,730	More than $28,730 but less than $34,470	More than $34,470 but less than $45,960	More than $45,960
Expected Family Contribution as a percent of income is	2.0%	3.0%	4.0%	6.3%	8.1%	9.5%	You pay full amount of premium.

Family Size = 2

If your income is	Less than $20,630	More than $20,630 but less than $23,270	More than $23,270 but less than $31,020	More than $31,020 but less than $38,780	More than $38,780 but less than $46,530	More than $46,530 but less than $62,040	More than $62,040
Expected Family Contribution as a percent of income is	2.0%	3.0%	4.0%	6.3%	8.1%	9.5%	You pay full amount of premium.

Family Size = 3

If your income is	Less than $25,970	More than $25,970 but less than $29,300	More than $29,300 but less than $39,060	More than $39,060 but less than $48,830	More than $48,830 but less than $58,590	More than $58,590 but less than $78,120	More than $78,120
Expected Family Contribution as a percent of income is	2.0%	3.0%	4.0%	6.3%	8.1%	9.5%	You pay full amount of premium.

(continued)

---

[3]Consumers Union. How Much Tax Do I Get? http://consumersunion.org/wp-content/uploads/2013/05/Tax_Credit_Worksheet_2014.pdf

Table 3-2. (continued)

Family Size = 4							
If your income is	Less than $31,320	More than $31,320 but less than $35,330	More than $35,330 but less than $47,100	More than $47,100 but less than $58,880	More than $58,880 but less than $70,650	More than $70,650 but less than $94,200	More than $94,200
Expected Family Contribution as a percent of income is	2.0%	3.0%	4.0%	6.3%	8.1%	9.5%	You pay full amount of premium.

Family Size = 5							
If your income is	Less than $36,670	More than $36,670 but less than $41,360	More than $41,360 but less than $55,140	More than $55,140 but less than $68,930	More than $68,930 but less than $82,710	More than $82,710 but less than $110,280	More than $110,280
Expected Family Contribution as a percent of income is	2.0%	3.0%	4.0%	6.3%	8.1%	9.5%	You pay full amount of premium.

According to the government, "Larger families [more than 5 members] may qualify for larger tax credits."

Again, the amount of the subsidy you'll receive is based on the cost of the premium for the second lowest-cost "silver" health plan available through your state's marketplace. (See Chapter 2 for more on this.) A silver plan will generally cover 70% of your medical costs, leaving the remaining 30% for you to pay.[4]

Although the size of your subsidy is calculated assuming you are buying a silver plan, you can choose to buy any of the other three types of health plans—a bronze plan, which will cover just 60% of your medical costs; a gold plan, which will on average pay for 80% of your costs; or a platinum plan, which will cover 90% of your medical costs.

---

[4]Community Catalyst & Georgetown University Health Policy Institute: What Are Federal Subsidies? http://101.communitycatalyst.org/aca_provisions/subsidies

Chapter 3 | Paying for Health Insurance

If you choose to buy a pricier health plan—gold or platinum—you'll be required to pay the difference between the credit you receive to help pay for your plan's premium and the cost of the more expensive plan. You can also choose to buy a less expensive plan, which will lower your premiums even further but offer less coverage for your medical care.[5]

In addition, some people will qualify for a price break on their out-of-pocket spending limits, such as deductibles, co-pays, and co-insurance.

To be eligible, your income must be less than roughly two and half times the poverty level, which is about $28,000 for an individual or about $58,000 for a family of four. However, you can take advantage of the subsidies to lower your out-of-pocket costs only when you buy a silver-level plan.[6]

Cost Alert Although premium tax subsidies can be applied to any of the "metal level" plans (bronze, silver, gold, platinum) sold through your state's marketplace, if you qualify, you can only take advantage of subsidies that lower your out-of-pocket costs (the amount you spend when you receive medical care) if you buy a silver-level plan.

Tables 3-3 and 3-4 shows out-of-pocket spending limits based on income for both individuals and families:

Table 3-3. Out-of-Pocket Spending Limits for an Individual[7]

Annual Income	Out-of-Pocket Costs by Percentage of Income	Percentage of Costs Covered by the Health Plan
Individuals		
$11,490–$15,282	2	94
$15,282–$17,235	3–4	94
$17,325–$22,980	4–6.3	87
$22,980–$28,725	6.3–8.1	73
$28,725–$34,470	8.1–9.5	70
$34,470–$40,215	9.5	70
$40,215–$45,960	9.5	70

---

[5]Ibid.
[6]Ibid.
[7]Center on Budget and Policy Priorities: Making Health Care More Affordable: The New Premium and Cost-Sharing Assistance: www.cbpp.org/cms/index.cfm?fa=view&id=3190

Table 3-4. Out-of-Pocket Spending Limits for a Family of Four[8]

Annual Income	Out-of-Pocket Costs by Percentage of Income	Percentage of Costs Covered by the Health Plan
Families of Four		
$23,550–$31,322	2	94
$31,322–$35,325	3–4	94
$35,325–$47,100	4–6.3	87
$47,100–$58,875	6.3–8.1	73
$58,875–$70,650	8.1–9.5	70
$70,650–$82,425	9.5	70
$82,425–$94,200	9.5	70

To understand the impact the subsidies can have on the cost of health insurance, let's take a look at individuals and families in five different scenarios and at how the tax credits will work when they buy insurance through their state's marketplace.

As I'll explain in detail later in this chapter, there are several ways to take the tax credits for which you're eligible. One option is to have the federal subsidies sent directly to your health plan so that you pay less each month for your policy.

Keep in mind the following are ballpark figures constructed with the use of the subsidy calculator available at the Kaiser Family Foundation's website (kff.org). To get firm prices for your insurance coverage, you will need to check with your state's marketplace.

Case Study 1

Name: John Richards

Age: 27

Marital status: Single, no children

Insurance type: Individual coverage

Annual income: $31,200 per year

---

[8]Ibid.

John's annual income	$31,200
The cost of health insurance without subsidies (annual cost)	$3,163
The subsidy John qualifies for	$456
John's cost for coverage after the subsidies are applied	$2,706 per year ($226 per month)

John's premium has been reduced by 14% for a silver-level health plan as a result of the tax credit.

If he chose to save even more money on his insurance premium, he could choose a bronze plan, priced at $2,165 a year or roughly $180 per month.

In addition, because John is younger than age 30, he can opt for a catastrophic health plan if one is sold through his state's marketplace. Again, these plans offer lower premiums but for considerably less coverage. In addition, individuals purchasing catastrophic plans are not eligible for premium tax credits. So, if John chooses this option, he will not get help from the federal government to lower either his premium or out-of-pocket costs.[9]

Case Study 2

Name: Beth Stone

Age: 44

Marital status: Single, two children younger than age 18

Insurance type: Family coverage

Annual income: $25,000 per year. If Beth and her two kids live in a state expanding Medicaid, she would qualify for the program. And because of Beth's income and the fact that her children are both younger than age 19, they would likely qualify for Medicaid or the Children's Health Insurance Program (CHIP). The CHIP program provides health coverage to children living in families with incomes too high to qualify for Medicaid, but that are unable to afford private health insurance.

If, however, Beth lives in a state not expanding its Medicaid program, here's how her insurance costs would be affected by the tax credits if she sought to buy coverage through her state's marketplace:

Beth's annual income	$25,000
The cost of health insurance without subsidies (annual cost)	$8,049
The subsidy Beth qualifies for	$7,549
Beth's cost for coverage after the subsidies are applied	$500 per year ($42 per month)

---

[9]Kaiser Family Foundation Health Insurance Subsidy Calculator.

In Beth's case, the government is covering 94% of the cost of her health insurance premium for a silver-level health plan.

She could bring her premium down to $0 per month by choosing to purchase a bronze plan instead.

In addition, Beth's income qualifies her for a break on out-of-pocket costs—the co-pays, co-insurance, and deductibles she must pay when she seeks medical care.

For a silver-level plan, which typically covers 70% of medical costs, Beth will instead receive coverage at about 94%, leaving her to pay the remaining 6% of costs when she goes to the doctor instead of 30%.

It should be noted, however, that if Beth chooses a bronze-level plan, she will not receive a break on out-of-pocket costs (the price break only applies to the premium). Those deductions only apply if she buys the silver plan.[10]

Case Study 3

Name: The Gonzalez Family

Age: Two adults, ages 38 and 36, and two children younger than age 18

Marital status: Married, two children

Insurance type: Family coverage

Annual income: $55,600 per year

The Gonzalez's annual income	$55,600
The cost of health insurance without subsidies (annual cost)	$11,306
The subsidy the Gonzalez family qualifies for	$7,101
The Gonzalez's cost for coverage after subsidies are applied	$4,205 per year ($350 per month)

This represents a price reduction of 63% for a silver-level health plan.

If the family chooses instead to buy a bronze plan, they would lower their premium to $2,270, or about $189 per month.

---

[10]Kaiser Family Foundation Health Insurance Subsidy Calculator.

In addition, the family's total income qualifies them for reduced out-of-pocket costs, which again, they can take advantage of only if they sign onto a silver-level plan.[11]

Case Study 4

Name: Judy and Rich Swanson

Age: 60 and 62

Marital status: Married, no children

Insurance type: Family coverage

Annual income: $31,000 per year

The Swanson's annual income	$31,000
The cost of health insurance without subsidies (annual cost)	$16,862
The subsidy the Swansons qualify for	$14,911
The Swansons cost for coverage after subsidies are applied	$1,951 per year ($163 per month)

This represents a price reduction of 88% for a silver-level health plan.

This couple could pay nothing on a monthly basis for health insurance if instead of a silver plan they bought a bronze-level plan.

However, the silver plan might be a better deal for this couple despite its higher monthly premium because their income entitles them to a subsidy to lower their out-of-pocket costs. Instead of a plan covering 70%, they would qualify for benefits that pay for 87% of their medical costs.[12]

Case Study 5

Name: The Bronsons

Age: 42 and 48

Marital status: Married, one child younger than the age of 18

Insurance type: Family coverage

Annual income: $110,000 per year

---

[11]Kaiser Family Foundation Health Insurance Subsidy Calculator.
[12]Kaiser Family Foundation Health Insurance Subsidy Calculator.

The Bronson's annual income	$110,000
The cost of health insurance without subsidies (annual cost)	$10,850
The subsidy the Bronsons qualify for	$0
The Bronsons cost for coverage after subsidies are applied	$10,850 per year ($904 per month)

This family's annual income is too high for them to qualify for a tax credit. This family would therefore be responsible for the full cost of their health insurance.

The Bronsons could, however, lower their cost by opting for a bronze-level health plan. The premium would drop by $1,857 a year (or by about $155 per month) to $8,993.[13]

Resource Alert You can learn how your health insurance premiums and out-of-pocket costs will be affected by using the Health Reform Calculator at the Kaiser Family Foundation's website: http://kff.org/interactive/subsidy-calculator/. You can also check on your state's health insurance marketplace. You can find your state's marketplace at Healthcare.gov.

No Other Offers of Coverage

In most cases, you won't qualify for a tax credit if your employer offers health insurance, even if you meet income requirements. However, the health plan offered by your employer does have to meet certain requirements:

- The premium cannot cost more than 9.5% of your annual income.
- Your employer's plan must pay for at least 60% of the cost of covered benefits.[14]

---

[13] Kaiser Family Foundation Health Insurance Subsidy Calculator.
[14] Kaiser Family Foundation. Focus on Health Reform: http://kaiserfamilyfoundation.files.wordpress.com/2011/04/8061-021.pdf

---

■ **Cost Alert!** **If your work-based insurance covers your spouse and/or children, take note!** The rules apply only to the cost of health insurance provided to the employee. If the plan costs less than 9.5% of the worker's income, family members will be able to buy insurance through the marketplace, but will not be eligible for subsidized coverage.

Where You Shop Matters

To take advantage of the price break you'll get from available tax credits, you must buy health insurance through your state's marketplace. You can start shopping October 1, 2013 for a health plan that will take effect January 1, 2014.

How to Take Your Tax Credit

We've talked a lot about the tax credits available under the law, and the various ways in which your costs may be reduced if you qualify. But how does the tax credit get applied? What do you have to do in order to take advantage of any savings to which you're entitled?

You have choices about how you take your tax credit: You can take it now, which will lower the amount of your monthly health insurance premium. In this case, the government will send the tax credit directly to your health plan. You can also pay the full premium during the year and take your credit at tax time. It's your choice.

The worksheet in Figure 3-1 shows you the impact of taking your tax credit now versus taking it when you file your tax return.

Healthcare, Insurance, and You

Two Ways to Take the Tax Credit — You Decide!

	Take It Now!		Take It Later!
October 2013 – March 2014	Sign up for health insurance at healthcare.gov • Tell them you want the tax credit "in advance" • Choose to take all your credit in advance — or just part of it	October 2013 – March 2014	Sign up for your health insurance at healthcare.gov
During 2014	• Pay a lower premium each month in 2014 — and now you are covered	During 2014	• Pay the full premium each month in 2014 — and now you are covered
January 2015 – April 2015	• Get a statement from your Health Insurance Marketplace showing how much tax credit you received in 2014 • File your 2014 taxes, including information about tax credit already taken	January 2015 – April 2015	• File your 2014 taxes • Subtract your tax credit from the tax you owe — or get a bigger refund if you don't owe anything
ADVANTAGE: Lower your health care premium each month!		ADVANTAGE: Lower the amount you pay at tax time!	

Jane needs to decide which way works best for her. Either way, she gets the same total tax credit for the year.

"If I take the tax credit now, I lower my monthly premium costs to $60."

Monthly Premium	$300
Monthly Tax Credit	– $240
New Monthly Cost	$60

"If I take the same tax credit later, I pay the full $300 premium now but get a bigger refund next April."

Tax Due	$900
Yearly Tax Credit	– $2,880
IRS Refund	$1,980

Figure 3-1. Two different ways to take your tax credit.
Source: Consumers Union.

There is, actually, one more alternative for taking your tax credit, and that is by taking a partial credit. For example, if you qualify for a credit that reduces your insurance premium by $200 per month, you can instead reduce your premium by $100 per month and claim the rest at tax time. Your monthly premiums will still be lower, just not by as much.

Because the tax credits are based on your income, changes that take place during the year because of a job loss, a change in your family situation, or an increase in salary can impact how much you'll owe in taxes at year's end. By taking some now and the rest at tax time, there is less chance of the need for repayment.

Reporting Changes

When changes to your income occur, you'll want to report them to your state's health insurance marketplace. Some of the changes to report are:

Changes in Family Size

- You get married or divorced.
- You have a baby.
- You no longer claim your child on your tax return.

Income Changes

- You get a raise.
- You lose your job.
- You take a salary cut.

An Offer of Health Insurance

- You're offered health insurance through a job.

Where to Get Help

All of this can be confusing. For information that pertains to your unique situation, keep these resources in mind:

- For details on whether you qualify and how much credit you will get, contact your state's health insurance marketplace at Healthcare.gov.
- At tax time, talk to your tax preparer or find free tax preparation help at irs.treasury.gov/freetaxprep, or call 1-800-906-9887.

Summary

The Affordable Care Act makes financial assistance available to millions of Americans with the goal of making health insurance more affordable. It's important to understand the new benefits available and how to take advantage of them so you don't miss out on an opportunity to gain access to benefits at a reduced cost.

In the next chapter we'll walk through the new benefits and rules the law puts in place for American businesses.

CHAPTER

4

Health Insurance at Work
The Impact of Obamacare on Your Benefits

The majority of Americans younger than the age of 65 who have health insurance—nearly 150 million people[1]— get their benefits at work. For most people, the Patient Protection and Affordable Care Act (ACA) isn't likely to change that. In fact, the extent of the law's impact on your work-based health insurance benefits will depend largely on the size of the company you work for. Those who either operate or work in a small business are likely to see the biggest changes.

The Role of Business

The majority of U.S. employers today offer health insurance benefits. Among firms with 200 or more employees, 98% provide workers with coverage, as do 94% of companies with 50 to 199 employees. Although small employers offer insurance at a much lower rate than large firms, most with 3 to 199 employees—61%—offer coverage as well.[2]

---

[1]University California Berkeley Labor Center. Summary of Provisions Affecting Employer-Sponsored Insurance: http://laborcenter.berkeley.edu/healthpolicy/ppaca12.pdf
[2]Kaiser Family Foundation. Snapshots: A Comparison of the Availability and Cost of Coverage for Workers in Small Firms and Large Firms: http://kff.org/private-insurance/issue-brief/snapshots-a-comparison-of-the-availability-and-cost-of-coverage-for-workers-in-small-firms-and-large-firms

On the whole, the benefits for which employers now pay are fairly generous. The Kaiser Family Foundation reports that in 2012:[3]

- A typical business with fewer than 200 employees paid 65% of family premiums that averaged $15,253 annually.
- Large employers with more than 200 employees paid 75% of a $15,980 family premium.

Although most companies already provide health benefits, employer-sponsored health insurance has been on a steady decline over the past decade. In 2000, nearly 70% of Americans got coverage on the job. By 2011, that number had shrunk to just 59.5%.[4] No doubt, rising costs are to blame. The price of family premiums has risen by 168% since 1999.

In an effort to offset this trend, the ACA was written to encourage employers to continue offering health insurance. But because the law makes generous premium tax credits and subsidies available to millions of Americans who don't have access to workplace benefits, the law's creators felt it was important to create incentives for employers to keep offering coverage and prevent them from shifting that responsibility to the government.

The fact that most employers in the United States already offer coverage means in practice the law doesn't represent a radical change in the current state of affairs—at least not for most Americans and for the foreseeable future.

The degree to which your health benefits will be impacted by the law, therefore, depends on whether you work for a large or a small company, whether you get health insurance at work today or don't. And if you are a business owner, the law may represent a change in whether and how you offer coverage to your employees.

---

[3]Kaiser Family Foundation. Snap Shot of a Comparison of the Availability and Cost of Coverage for Workers in Small Firms and Large Firms:
http://kff.org/private-insurance/issue-brief/snapshots-a-comparison-of-the-availability-and-cost-of-coverage-for-workers-in-small-firms-and-large-firms
[4]Robert Wood Johnson Foundation Report: Number of Americans Obtaining Health Insurance Declines Steadily Since 2000: http://www.rwjf.org/en/about-rwjf/newsroom/newsroom-content/2013/04/number-of-americans-obtaining-health-insurance-through-an-employ.html

Employers: ACA's Impact

When Congress set out to make health insurance available to all U.S. citizens, the architects of the ACA recognized that we could afford to do this only if we all share in the cost:

- Employers
- Employees
- Government, and
- The healthcare industry itself. The ACA will send millions of newly insured customers to hospitals, drug-makers, device-makers, and insurance companies—new customers who will be able to pay their bills. For this reason, the healthcare industry has agreed to taxes that will help fund the ACA.

"Shared responsibility" has become a major theme of reform.

Employer shared responsibility requires firms with 50 or more full-time workers to either provide health benefits or pay a penalty. The law defines "full-time employees" as those who work 30 or more hours a week.

Initially, this requirement was scheduled to begin January 1, 2014. However, during the summer of 2013, the Obama Administration announced a one-year delay, giving companies more time to prepare. Employers now have until 2015 to offer health benefits and to report to the Internal Revenue Service on details of the health insurance coverage they provide.[5]

In practice, this delay is not likely to have widespread impact on employee coverage because most employers have been offering insurance long before the ACA became law. In addition, a survey by consulting firm PricewaterhouseCoopers conducted soon after the government's announcement found that most private companies—more than 7 in 10—already consider themselves prepared for the next wave of ACA requirements.[6]

---

[5] U.S. Department of the Treasury website. July 2, 2013: Continuing to Implement the ACA in a Careful, Thoughtful Manner: http://www.treasury.gov/connect/blog/Pages/Continuing-to-Implement-the-ACA-in-a-Careful-Thoughtful-Manner-.aspx

[6] PricewaterhouseCoopers LLP. Majority of Private Companies Already in Compliance with Next Wave of Healthcare Reform Requirements, July, 2013: http://www.pwc.com/us/en/press-releases/2013/pwc-survey.jhtml

But the delay has encouraged a number of groups to lobby Washington in an effort to change the law's current definition of a full-time employee or "full-time equivalent" from one who works 30 hours to one who logs the more traditional 40-hour workweek.[7] Employers in industries that have not historically tracked the amount of time employees work by hours (home health nurses who are paid by the number of visits they make, for example), or who have a high percentage of seasonal or part-time workers—such as those in the retail, hotel, or restaurant industries—are most likely to be impacted by this.

If you work part time, therefore, this is an issue to watch, as any changes could impact whether you will have access to health insurance at work.

Penalties for Not Offering Health Benefits

Will your business or your employer be on the hook for a penalty? Here are the conditions under the law that can trigger a fine.[8]

- Say a company employing 50 or more full-time workers doesn't offer health benefits, and a full-time employee buys individual insurance through one of the state-based health insurance marketplaces and gets a tax credit from the government to help pay for it. In this case, the employer will pay a penalty of $2,000 per full-time employee (minus the first 30 workers).

- In a business that does offer insurance, if employees receive a tax break when they buy a health plan through the marketplaces, the employer is subject to a fine of as much as $3,000 for each full-time employee who buys the subsidized coverage (this is also minus the first 30 workers).

Figure 4-1 is a flow chart that outlines the penalties employers will face if they fail to offer health insurance to employees.[9]

---

[7]United States Department of Labor. Technical Release No. 2012-01: www.dol.gov/ebsa/newsroom/tr12-01.html
[8]Blumberg, L, et al. Urban Institute Health Policy Center. Implications of the Affordable Care Act for American Business: http://www.urban.org/UploadedPDF/412675-Implications-of-the-Affordable-Care-Act-for-American-Business.pdf
[9]Kaiser Family Foundation. Penalties for Employers Not Offering Affordable Coverage Under the Affordable Care Act Beginning in 2014: http://kaiserfamilyfoundation.files.wordpress.com/2013/04/employer_penalty_flowchart_1.pdf

Healthcare, Insurance, and You

Penalties for Employers Not Offering Affordable Coverage Under the Affordable Care Act Beginning in 2014

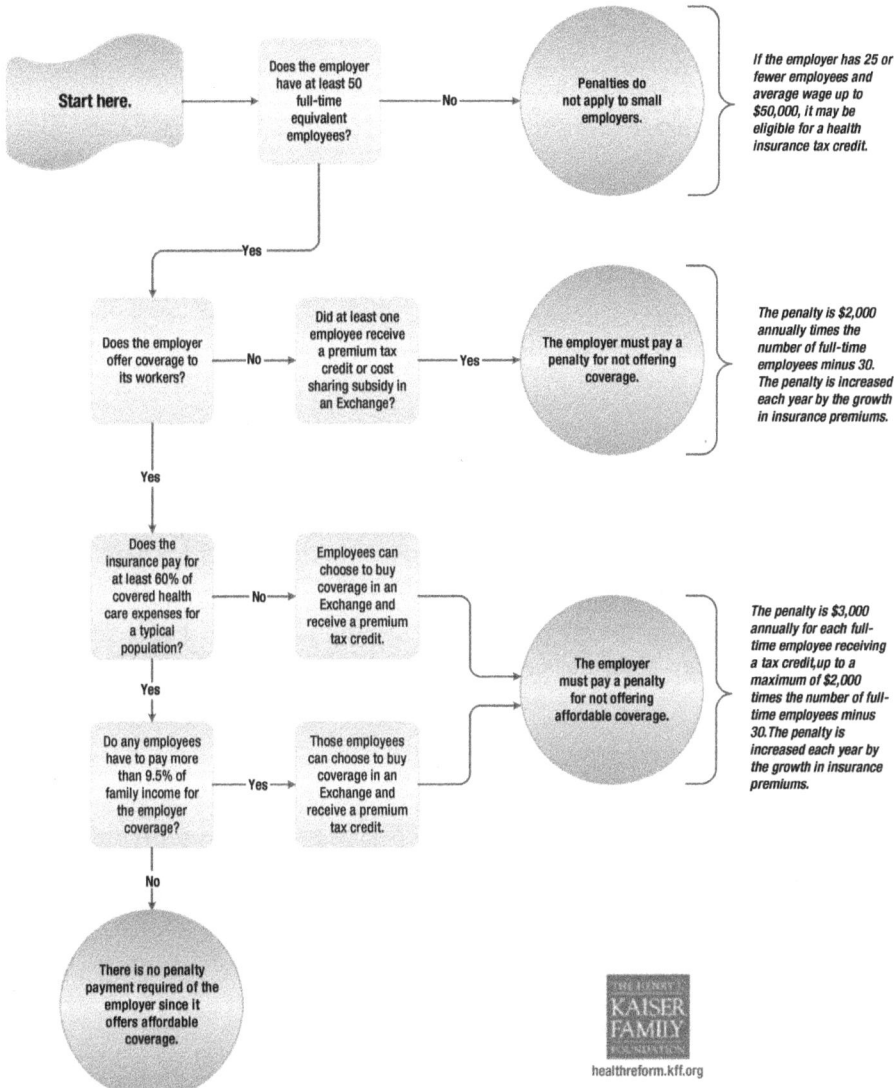

Figure 4-1. Penalties employers with 50 or more workers will pay if they fail to offer health benefits
Source: Kaiser Family Foundation. Used with permission

Employees: Health Benefits at Work

If you work for a company that already offers health insurance, there's a good chance you won't experience much change at all in your health benefits as a result of Obamacare.

However, if you work for a company with more than 50 employees that doesn't currently make health benefits available, your employer may decide to begin offering coverage to avoid having to pay penalties.

Here's what the law has in store.

New ACA Benefits Already in Place

Although the biggest changes being brought about by the ACA will take effect in 2014, there are a number of new benefits that have already been implemented.[10]

No More Lifetime Limits on Your Coverage

Before health reform, insurance companies were allowed to—and typically did—place a cap on how much money a policy would pay out for medical care before it stopped paying completely for any care.

Under the law, new insurance policies (those purchased after March 23, 2010) are prohibited from applying lifetime limits.

A Cap on Annual Limits

Annual limits on how much a health plan would pay toward your care were common prior to health reform as well. That's been limited by the law to anywhere between $1.25 million and $2 million depending on the start date of the plan. Beginning January 1, 2014, plans must eliminate annual dollar caps at the start of their new plan year.[11]

Preventive Care Is Covered

As I discussed in Chapter 1, the law has removed the cost of a number of preventive services. When you schedule an appointment for screenings for

---

[10] Berkeley Labor Center. Summary of Provisions Affecting Employer-Sponsored Insurance: http://laborcenter.berkeley.edu/healthpolicy/ppaca12.pdf
[11] Ibid.

colorectal and cervical cancers, lab workups for blood pressure and cholesterol levels, mammograms, immunizations such as flu shots, and well visits, you won't be on the hook for a deductible, co-payment, or co-insurance.

You can read about this in greater detail by referring back to Chapter 1. And, you can review a full list of covered preventive services at Healthcare.gov.

Tip When going for preventive health services pay close attention to the specific guidelines listed under each service on Healthcare.gov (and check with your insurer) to make sure the service is covered. For example, colonoscopies are a preventive service paid for in full by insurance if recommended by a physician for those age 50 and older. If you're younger than 50 or you need the exam because of a medical complaint, it likely won't be considered a "preventive" service and therefore, cost-free.

New Rights for Appealing Insurance Denials

Before the ACA became law, you may have had the right to appeal decisions made by your insurance company. For example, you might have been able to appeal denied authorization for treatment or refusal to pay for care you already received. However, some people did not have that right. Whether or not you did varied based on where you lived and the type of insurance you had. Under the new law, insurers must review their decision to deny paying for your care. If you are not satisfied with the outcome of that appeal, you now have the right to appeal a second time to an independent reviewer that does not work for the health plan.[12]

Children Can't Be Turned Down

As of September 23, 2010, new group policies cannot deny any child younger than the age of 19 a health plan, even if he or she has a pre-existing medical condition.

Young Adults Can Stay on Their Parents' Health Plan

The law now allows adult children to remain insured by their parents' health plan up to the age of 26, even if they don't live at home or reside in another state, are financially independent, or are married (this doesn't extend to the adult child's spouse). If the group health plan was in place on March 23, 2010, and the adult child has an offer of insurance through his or her job, signing on with a parent's insurance plan may not be an option. That restriction will end, however, on January 1, 2014.

---

[12]Families USA. Your Right to Appeal: www.familiesusa.org/health-reform-central/september-23/Your-Right-to-Appeal.pdf

As of the summer of 2013, about 3.4 million adult children received health insurance this way.[13]

A Limit on Waiting Periods

Under the law, your employer can't make you wait for a period of more than 90 days for your insurance plan to take effect.[14]

New Benefits and Changes Coming in 2014

There are additional requirements the law makes of employers (again, assuming you work for a company with 50 or more employees) that are scheduled to start January 1, 2014.[15]

Insurance Must Be "Affordable"

Your employer runs the risk of paying the government a penalty if the health insurance it offers isn't affordable. "Affordable" insurance means that no more than 9.5% of your annual household income goes toward the cost of your healthcare coverage.

It's important to note that even if you get family coverage through your employer, it's only the cost of *your* insurance—that of the employee—that counts, not the cost of family coverage.

In addition, the plan must pay, on average, 60% of medical costs covered by the plan. The affordability test applies to the lowest-cost health insurance option available to the employee that meets this minimum requirement.[16]

If either condition isn't met, your benefits do not meet the law's requirements for affordability. You would then be eligible to buy insurance through your state's health insurance marketplace, and if you qualify, receive a tax credit to help pay for it.

---

[13]Commonwealth Fund. Insuring the Future: Current Trends in Health Coverage and the Effects of Implementing the Affordable Care Act: http://www.commonwealthfund.org/Publications/Fund-Reports/2013/Apr/Insuring-the-Future.aspx
[14]Ibid.
[15]Berkeley Labor Center. Summary of Provisions Affecting Employer-Sponsored Insurance: http://laborcenter.berkeley.edu/healthpolicy/ppaca12.pdf
[16]Small Business Majority Health Coverage Guide: http://healthcoverageguide.org/affordable-care-act/shared-responsibility-requirements/#How+is+the+shared+responsibility+payment+calculated%3F

Determining Income Employers can use the income or wages reported on an employee's W-2 tax form to determine whether the cost of the workplace health plan is considered affordable under the ACA.[17]

The Cost of Insurance Is Limited

As discussed in Chapter 2, starting in January 2014, there are only three circumstances under which someone can be charged a higher rate for his or her health plan:

Age: Older people will pay a higher rate for coverage than the young, but the difference in price will be capped at a ratio of 3 to 1. That means someone age 62 won't pay more than three times what a 22-year-old pays for the same plan.

Geography: Insurers can factor geographic variations in the cost of providing medical services into their rates.

Tobacco use: The federal law allows insurers to charge people who smoke one and a half times more than non-smokers, though a handful of states have made it illegal for insurers to do so. And, if you smoke, you can minimize this surcharge by participating in a smoking cessation program.

These limits apply only to plans sold to small groups (and individuals) through the new small business marketplaces, which we'll discuss in detail later in this chapter.

Spending Is Limited

Health plans must limit how much you pay toward your out-of-pocket medical costs, including deductibles, co-pays, and co-insurance. In a given year, you can't be required to shell out more than to $6,350 for single coverage and $12,700 for a plan that covers families (2013 numbers). This amount does not include what you spend on your insurance premiums.

However, some group health plans have been granted a one year grace period that allows them to set higher or even no out-of-pocket limits on some medical costs. That means you could be required to spend more of your own funds for care in 2014. See Table 4-1 for more detail.

---

[17]United States Department of Labor. Technical Release 2012-01: www.dol.gov/ebsa/newsroom/tr12-01.html

Deductibles Are Limited

In the small group market (plans sold to businesses with fewer than 50 employees and eventually those with as many as 100 employees), health plan deductibles must generally be limited to $2,000 for single coverage and $4,000 for health plans covering families. Remember, the deductible is the amount you pay for medical services before your insurance begins to help pay the bills.

More Freedom and Protection

No longer can health plans require women to get a referral before seeing a doctor who specializes in obstetrics and/or gynecology (OB/GYN).

In addition, if you need emergency services, your health plan can't require you to obtain prior authorization before seeking care as a condition of coverage.

Finally, you can't be charged more for care received at the emergency department of a hospital that does not participate with your insurance plan network.

More Money Goes Toward Your Care

The law requires health plans to spend the bulk of the money they collect in premiums on medical services, rather than on marketing, executive salaries, or other administrative costs.

Large group health plans must spend at least 85% of premiums on medical services while small group health plans (those covering companies with fewer than 50 employees) must spend 80%. Anything less and they have to send a rebate either directly to consumers or to employers who can use the rebate to reduce insurance premiums for their workers.

Changes to Tax-Preferred Health Accounts

If along with your major medical benefits your employer offers you a Flexible Spending Arrangement (FSA), the law makes changes you should be aware of.

First, you can no longer use your FSA money for over-the-counter medications without a doctor's prescription. In addition, you cannot contribute more than $2,500 annually to these accounts.[18]

---

[18]Berkeley Labor Center. Summary of Provisions Affecting Employer-Sponsored Insurance.: http://laborcenter.berkeley.edu/healthpolicy/ppaca12.pdf

Health Plans and Employers That Get a Pass

Some of the new rules apply to all health plans and all employers. Others do not.

Most health plans offered by large firms, for example, are self-insured. That means the employer pays medical claims out of its own funds and contracts with an insurance company to administer the plan. These plans get a pass on certain parts of the law. For example, they aren't required to provide coverage that includes the 10 essential health benefits discussed in Chapters 1 and 2 (though most do anyway).

The rating rules—limits on how much more people can be charged for older age, tobacco use, and geography—don't apply either. And self-insured health plans are not required by law to comply with the limits on how high plan deductibles can be set.[19]

Jargon Alert *Self-insured* refers to a company that reimburses for health care expenses directly out of its own pocket. It hires an insurance company only to administer the plan. Typically, self-insured health plans are offered by large corporations with deep pockets.

Grandfathered health plans, those that were in place on or before March 23, 2010, are also exempt from having to comply with some parts of the law. Chapter 1 includes a chart showing which provisions in the ACA do and do not apply to grandfathered plans.

Table 4-1 outlines which parts of the ACA the different health plan types must comply with.

---

[19]Community Catalyst & Georgetown University Health Policy Institute, Health Insurance 101. Group Health Plans: http://101.communitycatalyst.org/basics/group_plans

Table 4-1. Standards for Employer-Sponsored Plans, by Plan Type

	Exchange plan	Grand-fathered plan	New employer-sponsored plan	Self-insured plan
No life time or annual limits: Plans are prohibited from limiting the lifetime dollar value of benefits effective now. Annual limits are currently restricted to between $1.25 million and $2 million depending on the plan year start date, and are banned completely beginning in 2014. Some plan shave been granted waivers to the annual limit requirements through 2013.	✓	✓ (annual limits do not apply to grandfathered individual plans)	✓	✓
Dependents under age 26: Plans must allow adult children under age 26 to enroll in a parent's plan effective now. Through 2013, adult children may only enroll in a parent's grandfathered plan if they are ineligible for another employer-sponsored plan.	✓	✓	✓	✓
Plan administrative costs: Plans must provide rebates to consumers if the percentage of premiums spent on medical services falls below 85 percent for large group plans or 80 percent for small group and individual plans (or higher standard set by state, if applicable) effective now.	✓	✓	✓	
Preventive services: Plans must offer first dollar coverage (no co-payment or deductible) for certain preventive services effective now.	✓		✓	✓
Patient protections: Plans are prohibited from requiring a referral to see an OB-GYN and from requiring prior authorization or higher cost sharing for out-of-network emergency services, effective now.	✓		✓	✓
Out-of-pocket maximums: Plans must limit out-of-pocket costs to $6,350 for single coverage and $12,700 for family coverage effective in 2014.*	✓		✓	✓
Pricing: Medical under writing is prohibited and rating variation is only allowed based on age (3:1 ratio), tobacco (1.5:1.0), family composition and geography effective in 2014.	✓		small group only	
Deductibles: Plans must limit deductibles to $2,000 for single coverage and $4,000 for family coverage beginning in 2014. Plans may exceed limit if they cannot reasonably reach the specified actuarial value.	small group only		small group only	
Minimum services covered: Plans must cover preventive and primary care, emergency, hospital, physician, outpatient, maternity and new born care, pediatric (including dental and vision), medical/surgical care, prescription drugs, lab, and mental health and substance abuse, effective in 2014. States set benchmarks within each category.	✓		small group only	

*Separate out-of-pocket limits for different services are allowed for plans beginning on or after January 1, 2014 and only for the first year. This will apply in cases when plans use multiple service providers to help administer benefits. For example, when a plan uses a third-party administrator for major medical coverage and a separate pharmacy benefit manager or managed behavioral health organization, there can be separate out-of-pocket limits for each service in 2014 that exceed $6,350 for an individual and $12,700 for a family. In future years, the out-of-pocket limits will have to be coordinated between service providers and stay within the limits set by the law.

Source: University California Berkeley Center for Labor Research and Education.

Expect Notice! Your employer must send you a notice about the health insurance marketplaces in your state and the premium tax credits available through the government (the marketplaces and premium tax credits are discussed in detail in Chapters 2 and 3). The company must also inform you that if you buy insurance on your own you may lose any contributions your firm makes to your health benefits. The notice needs to make its way to you by no later than October 1, 2013.[20]

Will My Insurance Costs Go Up?

The biggest concern people have about the impact of the ACA, understandably, is whether it's likely to increase their insurance costs. The answer to that question depends, at least in part, on the size of the company you work for.

Large Employers

Large employers are not bound by the law's essential health benefits requirements, nor are self-insured employers of any size. However, most already offer plans that cover those services and a rich menu of benefits. For that reason, Obamacare is not likely to lead to a hike in your insurance premiums if you work for and receive health benefits from a large firm. In fact, a 2012 report by the think tank Urban Institute found that the employer's cost of health benefits per person in companies with more than 1,000 employees remain virtually unchanged under the law.[21] And if your employer's costs remain unchanged, the portion you pay toward your benefits are likely to as well.

There is, however, one provision of the law that does have employers concerned about its potential to raise prices: The "Cadillac" tax.

Beginning in 2018, Employers and insurers that offer plans that cost more than $10,200 for an individual and $27,500 for a family will pay a 40% excise tax on the amount that exceeds these thresholds.

---

[20] United States Department of Labor. Guidance on the Notice to Employees of Coverage Options under Fair Labor Standards Act §18B and Updated Model Election Notice under the Consolidated Omnibus Budget Reconciliation Act of 1985: http://www.dol.gov/ebsa/newsroom/tr13-02.html
[21] Blumberg, L., et al., Urban Institute Health Policy Center. Implications of the Affordable Care Act for American Business: http://www.urban.org/UploadedPDF/412675-Implications-of-the-Affordable-Care-Act-for-American-Business.pdf

Many of these plans have such high premiums because they require very little cost-sharing of the enrollees (e.g., they may have a very small deductible or no deductible at all), they cover a broader than typical array of benefits, or they have very broad provider networks (some may have no provider network restrictions at all).

The impending Cadillac tax, along with a need to otherwise reduce health care costs, is leading many employers to alter the design of their benefits packages in a number of ways:

- **Higher costs for employees.** These may come in the form of deductibles, co-pays, and co-insurance (remember, unlike other health plans, large employers aren't bound to limits on the deductibles they can ask employees to pay).

- **Narrow provider networks.** This phrase refers to health plans with a limited selection of healthcare providers from which to seek care. If you wish to get the full level of reimbursement for your medical treatments, you'll need to stay in this network. Increasingly, employers are looking to lower their healthcare costs by carefully selecting doctors and hospitals that have proven their ability to provide high-quality medical care at competitive prices.

- **Wellness programs** have become increasingly popular with employers in recent years, and that's a trend that's expected to grow. The ACA allows employers to increase incentives for you to get involved in wellness programs at work by rewarding you 30% (up from 20% prior to the law) of the cost of your health coverage if you do. If you smoke and agree to participate in a smoking cessation program, your employer can offer incentives valued at as much as 50% of the cost of your benefits.[22]

---

[22]United States Department of Labor. The Affordable Care Act and Wellness Programs: http://www.dol.gov/ebsa/newsroom/fswellnessprogram.html

Mid-Sized Employers

A medium-sized company—one that employs between 101 and 1,000 employees, as defined by the Urban Institute report—can expect the cost of health insurance to rise. If you work for a company of this size, an increase in your employer's costs are likely to be passed along to you.

In this case, the Urban Institute study found that new ACA regulations with which businesses must comply would result in a rise in costs of about 4.6%—not a huge increase. To put that into perspective, it translates to the average annual amount an employer spends on benefits per employee jumping to $3,672 from $3,509—about $160 per year (2012 dollars).

However, much of that increase can be attributed to the penalties a mid-size employer would have to pay if it chooses not to offer health benefits. If your company currently offers coverage and plans to keep doing so, the increase in premium payments is much smaller—about $53 per insured person, or an increase of just 1.5%.

Small Employers

As I stated at the start of this chapter, it's the small employer that stands the most to gain under the health reform law. According to the Urban Institute report, overall, small firms (those with 100 or fewer employees) are likely to see a 7.3% drop in spending per insured person as a result of the ACA.

However, whether or not a small company sees cost savings is likely to vary for a host of reasons. Those with younger, healthier employees, for example, may see insurance rates that are higher than what they now pay. That's because starting in 2014, insurers will no longer be able to vary prices based on individual group members' health. Conversely, companies with older employees may see their prices drop for the same reason.

Small firms have historically faced a lot of inconsistency with regard to their insurance premiums. That's because a very sick employee one year or one lucky year in which few workers use health services has a big impact on the cost of insurance—much more so than for large firms where costs are spread over lots of people. The ACA's reforms are expected to create more stability in the price of small group premiums from one year to the next since the health risk in each year is spread over the entire small group insurance market.

This should make it easier for small businesses to plan for anticipated costs each year, and to stay in plans they like over time instead of getting a big premium spike and having to go search for a cheaper option.

Overall, early reports (in the summer of 2013) from states that released health plan prices for 2014 show lower rates in the small employer market that may be a result of increased competition among insurers.[23]

If You Own or Work for a Small Business

The biggest misconception about the ACA is that it requires small business owners to provide health insurance to their employees. It doesn't. Any business with 50 or fewer full-time employees is exempt from the employer mandate and not required to provide workers with health insurance. Small businesses also will not be subject to fines, whether or not they offer their workers coverage.

Note Small businesses, those with 50 or fewer employees, are not required to provide health insurance to members of their workforce. And that's 95% of all employers in the United States.

That means that the majority of American businesses will not be required to offer employee health benefits. According to the Congressional Budget Office, 95% of all firms in the United States have fewer than 50 employees.[24]

Many small business owners want to provide health insurance, but have been priced out of the market. Insurance tends to be costlier for small businesses because of administrative expenses that are higher than for large employers, and in most states insurers are allowed to charge higher premiums based on the age and health status of employees.

And, as mentioned earlier, because small firms have fewer employees to absorb the financial risk of high medical expenses, those with older or sicker workers can face steep premiums. And one employee facing a serious illness can cause an increase in premiums for the whole company the following year.

This accounts for the lower rates at which small businesses offer health insurance as compared with large firms. Only 50% of businesses with fewer than 10 employees make health benefits available to their workers, according to the Kaiser Family Foundation.[25] That number has been steadily shrinking over the past decade.

---

[23]The Commonwealth Fund. State Action Round-Up on Affordable Care Act Implementation: http://www.commonwealthfund.org/Blog/2013/Jul/State-Action-Roundup-July-19.aspx?omnicid=20
[24]Congressional Budget Office. Small Firms, Employment and Federal Policy: http://www.cbo.gov/sites/default/files/cbofiles/attachments/SmallFirms_0.pdf
[25]Kaiser Family Foundation. 2012 Employer Health Benefits Survey: http://kff.org/report-section/ehbs-2012-section-2

The ACA puts in place a number of new structures and rules intended to make health benefits more affordable for small businesses and to have a wider selection of health plans from which to choose.

Shop Exchanges

In Chapter 2, I talked at length about the new health insurance marketplaces, or exchanges, where individuals will be able to compare health plans, learn if they qualify for a tax credit, and ultimately sign up for a plan.

The law also calls for the creation of a second type of insurance exchange for small businesses: The Small Business Health Options Program (SHOP). The SHOP exchanges will be open for business starting October 1, 2013.

For 2014, only companies with fewer than 50 employees will be able to purchase coverage for their workers via the SHOP exchange. By 2016, firms with 100 full-time employees will also be allowed to participate in these new markets, and starting in 2017, states have the option of expanding access to even larger businesses.[26]

The idea behind SHOP exchanges is to offer business owners and their employees a choice of qualified health plans and to enable them to easily compare health plans online and select from a variety of options. However, employers can also purchase insurance that meets the law's standards outside of the SHOP exchange if they choose.[27]

The following sections explain how it all works.

Standardized Plans

All plans sold to small businesses must offer the same set of "essential health benefits" (the full list can be found in Chapter 2). And, as mentioned earlier, plans sold to small businesses must limit annual deductibles to $2,000 for individual coverage and $4,000 for family coverage. As with all other health plans, maximum out-of-pocket costs must be limited to $6,350 for individuals and $12,700 for families.

---

[26]UC Berkeley Labor Center. Summary of Provisions Affecting Employer-Sponsored Insurance. http://laborcenter.berkeley.edu/healthpolicy/ppaca12.pdf
[27]Kaiser Family Foundation. Explaining Health Reform: How Will the Affordable Care Act Affect Small Businesses and Their Employees? http://kff.org/health-reform/fact-sheet/explaining-health-reform-how-will-the-affordable-care-act-affect-small-businesses-and-their-employees/

The plans will be broken out into "metal levels," which vary by the percentage of medical costs covered:

- Bronze (60%)
- Silver (70%)
- Gold (80%)
- Platinum (90%)

Everyone Is Approved

Insurers can no longer turn anyone away for coverage or charge more for pre-existing health conditions. That means if an employee gets sick and uses a lot of medical services, premium costs won't spike the following year for the group, as they often do in today's small-group market.[28]

Employee Choice

The law has been written to give small business owners the ability to decide how much money they wish to contribute toward their employees' benefits. Then workers will be able to go onto the SHOP exchange and select from among a number of health plan options, and apply their employer's financial contribution to the plan they feel best meets their needs.

However, this is another provision of the law that has been delayed by one year. Instead of giving small businesses multiple health plans options, in 2014, employers in most states will have access only to the one plan selected for them by their employer.[29]

The SHOP exchanges will have tools available to help you. The government has created a website to help business owners explore and understand their health insurance options under the law at Business.USA.gov/healthcare.

If you live in a state operating its own SHOP exchange, employees of small firms may have the ability to choose from among a number of available plans being sold for 2014—rather than just one plan option, as will be the case for states with a SHOP marketplace run by the federal government. Log onto Healthcare.gov, Business.USA.gov/healthcare or see the Appendix for your state's contact information to learn how this will be handled where you live. By 2015, employee choice is expected to be available throughout the country.

---

[28]Healthcare.gov. What Do Small Businesses Need to Know.
[29]California Healthline. Obama Administration Delays Rollout of ACA's Small Business Program: http://www.californiahealthline.org/articles/2013/4/2/obama-administration-delays-rollout-of-acas-small-business-program

Where choice is available, generally, small business owners may choose a tier of coverage from which employees can select a plan—bronze, silver, gold, or platinum-level plans. If you're a small business owner, you'll also decide how much you wish to contribute to the cost of your employees' health benefits. Employees can then log onto the SHOP exchange and choose any plan within the tier of coverage you select.

Brokers Welcome

If you have an established relationship with a licensed insurance broker or simply prefer working with one for personal assistance in reviewing and selecting a health plan that meets your employees' needs and your budget, you may do so. This will not add any cost to the insurance plan(s) you select.

Tip To find a broker in your area you can search the website of the National Association of Insurance Commissioners (www.naic.org) or at eHealthInsurance.com. You can also contact them by phone at: 1-800-977-8860.

Everyone Must Be Included

Small business owners who decide to purchase health benefits through their state's SHOP exchange are required to extend that coverage to all full-time employees (those who work an average of 30 or more hours per week). And, in many states, at least 70% of a firm's full-time employees must enroll in the employer's SHOP plan.

A company's insurance application will be held until the employer meets the 70% minimum participation requirement (or meets the requirement for the state in which it operates) (see Healthcare.gov).[30]

Tallying Employees' Time

Business owners will need to know how many of their employees are considered full-time under the law. There are nuances associated with accurately determining that number. Depending on the type of company you run and the workers you employ, this can be complicated.

---

[30]Centers for Medicaid and Medicare Services. FF-SHOP Issuer Frequently Asked Questions: https://www.regtap.info/uploads/library/SHOP_Issuer_FAQs2_5CR_070813.pdf

However, here is a snap shot of what you need to know about how to tally the number of employees working for your business:

- When it comes to determining who works full-time for the purposes of complying with the law, the government counts hours. Employees who work 30 hours per week or more (or an average of 130 paid hours per month, including vacations, holidays, and sick days) are full-time and eligible for health benefits if they're offered.

- To determine whether your business will be subject to fines if it fails to provide employee health benefits, look at the size of your workforce during the prior calendar year.

- To calculate the number of full-time equivalent employees, divide the total hours worked by non-full-time employees in a month and divide by 120.[31]

- Even though part-time workers count toward the total number of employees eligible for health benefits, the law doesn't mandate businesses to offer part-time workers insurance coverage.[32]

- There can be variations in how the calculations must be figured in states operating their own SHOP marketplace. Each state's insurance application will outline how to count full-time employees to determine who is eligible for SHOP coverage.

- Companies with employees in more than one state in most cases may establish either one SHOP account that serves all its locations, or set up accounts in each state where employees are based. With just one account employees in all states will be included when calculating an employer's SHOP participation rate. With multiple accounts, employees in each state will be counted separately.[33]

- You can use the two-step process outlined in Figure 4-2 below to assist you in determining if your business will be held responsible for providing employee health benefits.

---

[31]Ibid.
[32]Healthcare.gov. What Is the Shop Marketplace?
[33]Centers for Medicaid and Medicare Services. FF-SHOP Issuer Frequently Asked Questions: https://www.regtap.info/uploads/library/SHOP_Issuer_FAQs2_5CR_070813.pdf

Healthcare, Insurance, and You

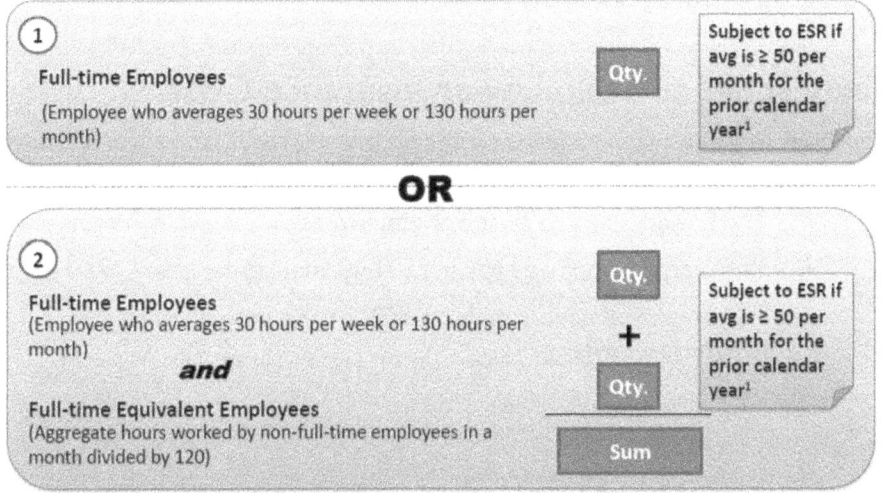

Figure 4-2. Two-step process to determine if you are responsible for providing employee benefits. Source: U.S. Small Business Administration, Affordable Care Act 201: Employer Shared Responsibility Provisions, July 2013.

Fluctuating Hours

One point of major confusion for businesses when tallying the number of hours an employee works is in cases when hours fluctuate and/or an employee switches from full-time to part-time work.

The law allows business owners to use a "look-back" period of 3 to 12 months during which the employee's hours would be averaged. That look-back period would then be followed by a stability period likely of the same length. If the hours worked by an employee averaged 30 hours or more per week, the business would be required under the law to provide that worker coverage to avoid a penalty.

---

[34] *New York Times.* You're The Boss: The I.R.S. Interprets the Employer Mandate, and Businesses Have Questions. July 23, 2013 by Robb Mandelbaum.

However, the rules are not only confusing, there are also details yet to be worked out by the Internal Revenue Service about how businesses can and should proceed in the case of fluctuating hours. You can expect final decisions to be made during 2014.[34]

Tax Credits to Help Lower Insurance Costs

The ACA helps to make health insurance more affordable for small business owners by offering tax credits as long as:

- The business has 25 or fewer employees
- The average employee pay is $50,000 annually or less
- The employer covers at least 50% of the cost of single health care coverage[35]

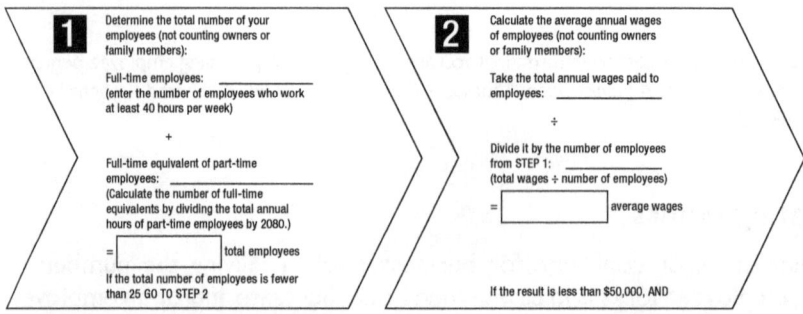

Figure 4-3. Steps to figure out if you are able to claim the Small Business Health Tax Credit
Source: IRS.gov

---

[35]Internal Revenue Service. Small Business Health Care Tax Credit for Small Employers: http://www.irs.gov/uac/Small-Business-Health-Care-Tax-Credit-for-Small-Employers
[36]Ibid.

If the business fits this profile, starting in 2014 the government will offer tax credits of up to 50% for small businesses and 35% for tax-exempt employers, such as charities.[36]

The credit works on a sliding scale with smaller companies standing the most to gain.

You can use the three-step process outlined in Figure 4-3 to determine if your business will qualify for a tax credit by offering employee health benefits.

Wellness Program Grants

If you operate a business with fewer than 100 employees who work 25 or more hours per week on average, there are incentives for starting a workplace wellness program.[37]

To qualify for grants available to establish a work-based wellness program, a company cannot have had a program already in place when the ACA became law in March, 2010. You can find more information about the grants at the Centers for Disease Control and Prevention (http://www.cdc.gov/nationalhealthyworksite/index.html).

Should You Offer Insurance to Your Employees?

If you are a small business owner with fewer than 50 employees and thinking about whether to offer employee health benefits, there are a number of things to consider when determining the best course of action. Remember, for you, offering insurance is an option, not a requirement under the ACA.

What's Your Business?

Health benefits have long been used by businesses as a tool for recruiting and retaining workers. If your business is composed mainly of owners—such as physician offices, attorney and CPA firms—it's likely to be advantageous to offer coverage, largely because work-based health insurance is tax deductible. It also makes sense for a business needing to attract highly skilled workers.

---

[37]Kaiser Family Foundation. Explaining Health Reform: How will the Affordable Care Act Affect Small Businesses and their Employees? http://kff.org/health-reform/fact-sheet/explaining-health-reform-how-will-the-affordable-care-act-affect-small-businesses-and-their-employees/

Offering insurance may make less sense for restaurants or other businesses with a significant number of minimum wage or unskilled workers.

The Impact of Tax Credits

As discussed earlier, some small businesses will qualify for tax credits. If your business is among them, ask yourself if they are significant enough to make it worthwhile to offer health benefits to employees. You'll need to do the math.

Your Employees' Attitudes toward Coverage

Because employer-sponsored health insurance has been the primary source of health benefits for people younger than the age of 65 for so long in this country, employees newly required to have health insurance under the law may prefer to get coverage at work. If offering coverage is very important to your employees, it's worth looking at whether you can reasonably do so.

Think about Your Workers' Wallets

In some cases, most employees might qualify for tax credits and subsidies by buying insurance on their own through the individual health insurance marketplaces being set up under the law. It's possible that it may be in your employees' best financial interest to buy coverage on their own rather than get it at work.

Again, it's important to do the math. How much, on average, do your employees earn? And, how much of a tax credit will they qualify for if they were to buy individual coverage? In some cases, they may get a better deal going it alone.

Summary

The Affordable Care Act uses both carrots and sticks when it comes to encouraging employers to offer workplace health benefits. For most Americans the law won't have a large impact on their coverage, at least not in the short term. It's really owners and employees of small businesses that will see new benefit designs and richer packages than they likely see today, and who stand to gain from the financial assistance being made available by the government. In addition, small firms are likely to benefit from the new SHOP marketplaces, which are expected to help stabilize insurance premiums for this segment.

In the next chapters, we'll talk about healthcare costs and how to navigate the insurance benefits you have to get the best possible care while avoiding common costly mistakes.

CHAPTER 5

Cutting Medical Costs
Avoiding Common, Pricey Mistakes

Healthcare in the United States is pricey. And if it seems like it's getting harder to afford the medical care and health insurance you need, it's not your imagination.

Healthcare Is Getting More Expensive

In the United States, the cost of healthcare—the amount of money spent on doctor visits, hospital stays, and treatments—rose by 131% between 1999 and 2009, far greater than prices in the rest of the economy.

Health insurance premiums have been rapidly on the rise too. Between 2002 and 2012, families have seen the cost of their health insurance rise by an average of 102%. Yet, during that same period, earnings grew by just 33%.[1]

---

[1] Kaiser Family Foundation: Employer Health Benefits Summary 2012: http://ehbs.kff.org/pdf/2012/8346.pdf

Not only do prices rise at breakneck speed, but you, the healthcare consumer, are also on the hook for a growing portion of those costs. And, that's a trend that's expected to continue.

If you get your insurance at work, you've no doubt noticed over the years that your employer has asked you to pay a bigger share of your premiums. Other costs are higher too; co-pays, co-insurance, and deductibles are more expensive for many people than they once were. More and more, employers who offer workers health benefits are in search of ways to manage the ever growing cost of healthcare. One way they're doing this is by shifting costs to you, the employee. And though people who buy insurance on their own will gain new protections under the Affordable Care Act, including annual limits to how much they'll be required to spend on their medical care, total out-of-pocket costs may still be high.

Your Benefits Look Different

As the cost of health insurance has gotten more expensive, high-deductible health plans have grown in popularity. This type of health insurance comes with monthly premiums that are lower than conventional insurance coverage. On average, high-deductible health plans cost about 15% less than traditional health plans. That's the good news. The downside is they require consumers to pay thousands of dollars more in out-of-pocket expenses when they go for medical care.

These plans are on the rise. In 2006 just 4% of Americans who got their health benefits at work were enrolled in a high-deductible plan. Today, that number is roughly 19%, and the market is expected to continue growing.[2] Nearly half of all people who buy insurance on their own are enrolled in a high-deductible health plan.

The fact is that employers who provide employee health coverage save money when employees choose to sign onto high-deductible plans as compared with more traditional coverage. It's a way of shifting costs from their books to yours.

---

[2]Kaiser Family Foundation: Employer Health Benefits Summary 2012.

But there's another rationale supporting the growth of the high-deductible health plan: When people are forced to shell out their own hard-earned cash for something, they choose what they will and won't buy more carefully. This means that if instead of simply paying $10 to see your doctor you have to cover the full $250 for the visit, you're likely to think more carefully about how essential that visit is to you. And, the thinking goes, you'll have a greater incentive to shop around for the best price on healthcare services, which overall will help to decrease unnecessary care and ultimately lower costs.

But does it work out that way?

Hidden Healthcare Prices

Studies show that more than 6 in 10 patients don't know the cost of their care until the bill arrives.[3]

One likely reason for this is that finding the prices of medical services has, historically, been a nearly impossible task.

Here's a basic fact you need to understand about healthcare pricing: Not everyone pays the same amount for the same service. What you pay to see your doctor or to get a magnetic resonance imaging (MRI) or computed tomography (CT) scan depends on whether or not you have health insurance, and if so, what type of insurance you have. Contracts between healthcare providers, such as doctors and hospitals, and insurance companies are based on negotiated discounts, and no two prices look alike.

If you have insurance and go to a doctor who's contracted with your health plan, you'll pay a portion of the rate your insurer negotiated with your doctor.

Ironically, if you don't have insurance, you'll be charged a higher price than those who do have it—in some cases, as much as 1000% more!

Without the negotiating muscle of an insurance company behind you, you're left to pay the full cost of your doctor's charges. Think of it like paying the full sticker price listed on a new car.

Costs Can Get in the Way of Treatment

The other problem many people with high-deductible health plans face is that although some folks—mostly those who are healthy and don't need a lot of medical care—save money by lowering their monthly insurance premiums,

---

[3]Aetna. Decision 2012: Healthcare Benefits Second Most Difficult Decision for Consumers: http://bit.ly/Vv8k4S

studies have shown that more often than not, people with chronic illness tend to delay, or in some cases skip getting care completely. For millions of Americans, money—or a lack thereof—gets in the way of their ability to take care of their medical needs.[4]

Whether you think it's a good idea for patients to be on the hook for more of their medical costs or not, the trend is here to stay. That means if you're not covered by a high-deductible health plan now, you may very well be at some time in the near future.

With deductibles that average about $2,200 for individuals and $4,000 for families (in 2012), and annual out-of-pocket costs capped at about $6,000 for single coverage and $12,000 for family coverage, you'll need to prepare yourself to shell out more of your hard-earned dollars on medical care.[5] Even if you have a more traditional type of health plan, you've likely seen your portion of your premiums, co-pays, and deductibles rise.

You can't control the larger market forces in healthcare. And, if you are suddenly hit with a major illness, you aren't left much choice about getting treatment to save your life or improve your health. But that doesn't mean all control is out of your hands. The key is to be armed with the right information to make smarter choices that can help you gain access to needed medical care and save money in the process.

As the old maxim goes: Knowledge is power.

Avoiding Common, Costly Mistakes

How well do you understand the details of your insurance plan?

If you're like most Americans, the answer is not very well. Industry surveys have found that most people—nearly 90%, in fact—feel that information about their health benefits is utterly confusing. And, many have no idea how much money they spend on their healthcare in a given year in out-of-pocket expenses.[6]

Understanding the basics of your health plan can have major financial consequences. In addition, knowing what pitfalls to avoid can make a significant difference in the cost of your medical care.

---

[4]Galbraith, Soumerai, Ross-Degnan, Rosenthal, Gay, and Lieu. Delayed and Forgone Care for Families with Chronic Conditions in High-Deductible Health Plans, *Journal of General Internal Medicine*, 27(9):1105–11. DOI: 10.1007/s11606-011-1970-8.
[5]Kaiser Family Foundation: Employer Health Benefits 2012 Annual Survey
[6]Aetna. Decision 2012: Healthcare Benefits Second Most Difficult Decision for Consumers: http://bit.ly/Vv8k4S

Mistake: Failing to Follow Your Health Plan's Rules

You pay every month for the privilege of having insurance coverage, but that doesn't mean you're in charge. When it comes time to use your health benefits, you either play by your insurer's rules or risk losing financial coverage for the care you receive. Even worse, failing to use your benefits correctly can block you from getting the healthcare you need.

The Fix: Do Your Research

It sounds simple—do your research and know the details of your health plan—but insurance is a topic that can confuse even the savviest among us. And let's face it—reading your health plan benefit details is about as interesting as watching paint dry.

Still, the only way to guarantee that your doctor visit, hospital stay, medication, or test is going to be covered by insurance is by understanding what's allowed under the terms of your plan.

Ask yourself the following questions before going for care:

- Does my plan require me to see healthcare providers who are "in-network?"

- Do I need prior authorization from my insurer before I buy medication or go to see a specialist? Call your insurer and ask if you don't know.

- Am I required to try another less expensive medication before my insurer will agree to pay for the name-brand version my doctor ordered?

- Does my plan place limits on what it will pay for lab work and other diagnostic testing, mental health, chiropractic services, or inpatient hospital care?

The good news is that you don't need to read your entire insurance booklet in one sitting. The key is to get into the habit of checking with your insurance company or your benefits manager at work to clarify what is and isn't covered by your health plan, and what steps, if any, you must take before getting care. That's one of the best ways to maximize your coverage and avoid surprise medical bills.

Mistake: You Do Everything Your Doctor Tells You To

For many people, questioning the medical care their doctor suggests is considered an act of defiance and one they'd be apprehensive to take. In fact, research has shown that even highly educated, affluent people who feel assertive in other parts of their lives feel anxious about challenging their doctors. It even makes them nervous to ask too many questions for fear of being seen as difficult or disrespectful and that their doctor's negative perception will then lead to subpar care.[7]

Yet, the fact is that many patients are recommended treatment that isn't necessary. In fact, according to the nonprofit Institute of Medicine, more than $200 billion is wasted in the United States each year on unnecessary medical services.[8]

Not only can avoiding unnecessary care be better for your health, but it's also the best way to save money.

The Fix: Learn to Ask Questions

Start to get comfortable asking your physician questions. Here are some to consider:

- What will this test tell you about my condition?
- Is this test/procedure the only option to gain the information you're after?
- Is this medication covered by my insurance plan?
- Is there a less expensive option?

By asking questions about the care being suggested, including those that address costs, you will open up a dialogue between you and your doctor. It's likely to lead you to a better understanding of your medical treatment and alert your doctor to the fact that, although your health is a priority, you can't care for yourself properly if you're unable to afford what is being prescribed.

Before agreeing to further tests or treatment, I highly recommend you take a look at the website www.choosingwisely.org. Choosing Wisely is a campaign backed by many of the country's medical academies to alert both patients and doctors to medical treatments that are commonly recommended but more

---

[7]Frosch, May, Rendle, Tietbohl, and Elwyn. Authoritarian Physicians and Patients' Fear of Being Labeled "Difficult" Among Key Obstacles to Shared Decision Making, *Health Affairs*: http://content.healthaffairs.org/content/31/5/1030.abstract

[8]Institute of Medicine: http://resources.iom.edu/widgets/vsrt/healthcare-waste.html

often than not are unnecessary and sometimes cause harm. They also often lead to unnecessary costs. As this book goes to press, there were more than 200 tests and procedures listed as those that patients should question their doctors about before proceeding.

These are some of the tests to skip: imaging tests for low-risk ovarian cysts, a colonoscopy more than once every 5 or 10 years if you don't have risk factors for colon cancer, an annual Pap test for women at low risk of cervical cancer, and the use of antibiotics to treat sinusitis.

> **Tip** Head to www.choosingwisely.org before following your doctor's advice blindly.

Mistake: You Don't Check Your Doctor's Provider Status

Is he or she in or out? That's the first question you need to ask and answer about your doctor's status in your health insurer's provider network.

An in-network doctor is a physician who has signed a contract agreeing to accept patients with your type of insurance *and* to accept an agreed-on rate for providing them medical care.

The Fix: Check Directly with Your Doctor

Getting care from an in-network doctor, lab, or hospital will cost you less money than going to one that is out-of-network. In addition, should a dispute occur over cost or other issues, you'll have greater protections and back-up support from your insurer in your efforts to resolve them. So you have to check your provider's status *before* you go for a visit or have surgery.

If you're having surgery, remember that everyone treating you while you're hospitalized needs to be in-network in order for you to receive full coverage. But the reality is, that's a tall order, and even patients who have made every effort to stay in-network are sent large bills after a hospital stay from doctors who treated them but don't participate with their insurance plan.

Still, make an effort to minimize possible sticker shock by checking with the hospital, your doctor, and your anesthesiologist, and talk with hospital administration in advance to see what can be done to minimize the risk of being charged for out-of-network care provided during your hospital stay.

And here's an important tip: don't rely on your insurance company's website or your benefits booklet for your doctor's network status. Provider networks change all the time, and insurers' websites are notoriously out of date with regard to their network of participating providers. Always call the doctor's office in advance to confirm that he or she participates with your health plan.

Also, it's important to be precise about the way you ask the question. Patients commonly run into trouble by asking if their insurance is accepted. The answer "yes," in this case, often gives patients the false impression that the provider is considered in-network. This is not necessarily so.

Doctors and hospitals often accept payment from insurers when a patient's policy is a preferred provider organization plan (PPO) that reimburses for out-of-network care. But that doesn't mean they're contracted with the insurers and will accept their rates. If you go to an out-of-network doctor without realizing it, you're sure to be hit with a surprise bill a few weeks down the road that is much higher than what you expected. The question you must ask to confirm a provider's participation in your insurer's network, therefore, is: "Are you contracted with my insurer as an in-network provider?"

Mistake: You Misunderstand How Your Insurer Reimburses for Out-of-Network Care

Insurance companies, in case you haven't noticed, can be sneaky. As a way of saving money, they've started to change the way they reimburse for out-of-network medical services.

Here's how it used to work: Insurers paid a percentage of what's called usual, customary, and reasonable (UCR) charges. UCR rate are a base amount insurers use to calculate how much they will pay for services that are reimbursed by the plan. If your policy reimburses for out-of-network care, the payment will be based on a price that your insurer determines to be "usual, customary and reasonable" in your area. So, if your last visit to the doctor cost $200 and your insurer pays 70% of your out-of-network costs, you'd be reimbursed $140 and owe the remaining $60 (this assumes that you've already met your deductible). Of course, your insurer may determine that UCR for the service is only $180, not the $200 your doctor charged. In that case, you would only be reimbursed 70% of $180, or $126.

Insurers have now added a new twist. Instead of reimbursing UCR charges, they've started to pay based on Medicare rates. Medicare rates are typically lower than UCR, which means your insurer pays you less money for your care and you are stuck with a bigger bill than you expected.

The Fix: Read the Fine Print

We'll talk more about the issue of prices for healthcare services later in this chapter. Suffice it to say that consumers are getting a raw deal: As we move to high-deductible health plans and patients have a greater need than ever to know what their care will cost, they find those numbers are extremely hard, if not impossible, to find.

You likely aren't used to asking about the cost of your medical care, but it's something you need to get comfortable doing if you're to avoid excessive costs you didn't plan for.

The way in which health plans reimburse can vary, and it can get confusing to figure out how your particular plan operates. Here's an example of what I mean: If your health plan uses the Medicare-based formulas mentioned above, you may learn that you'll be reimbursed at a rate of 110% to 140% of Medicare fees. Reimbursed at 110% of your costs—well, that sounds like a good deal! But don't get excited just yet.

If your insurer, on the other hand, reimburses the more traditional UCR rates, often it does so at a rate of 70% or 80% for out-of-network medical care.

On the face of it, it would be natural to assume that a formula reimbursing you at a rate of 110% would be the more generous deal for you than being reimbursed at just 80%. But you'd likely be wrong. Why? It's because UCR rates are higher than Medicare rates.

To illustrate my point, let's take a common medical procedure, such as a colonoscopy, during which you're placed under anesthesia and a biopsy is conducted.

When UCR standards apply, the patient's cost for the procedure would come to $631.78. If a Medicare formula is applied the very same procedure will cost you $1,319.77. That's a difference of $687.99![9]

Mistake: You Assume Your Bills Are Correct

Nearly 10% of medical claims processed by health insurance companies are inaccurate, according to the American Medical Association. Other groups have claimed that as many as 8 in 10 medical bills are wrong.[10,11]

The moral of this story is: You cannot trust that the bills sent to you by doctors and hospitals are accurate, or that your insurance company has paid a claim properly.

The Fix: Check for Billing Errors and Fight Back

Request an itemized bill, particularly if you've recently been hospitalized, and look carefully for a number of common errors:

- Duplicate charges
- Services that were not provided, such as doctor visits or tests

---

[9] Fair Health Consumer Cost Look Up: http://bit.ly/n86cbS
[10] American Medical Association: http://bit.ly/jtCi2m
[11] Medical Billing Advocates of America: http://bit.ly/UkNBnT

- Supplies that are supposed to be included in the price of the hospital room (gloves, drapes, sutures, and cotton balls)
- Care provided by out-of-network doctors you didn't agree to see while hospitalized

If anything looks fishy, get ready to fight the charges. I'll discuss fighting medical bills in greater detail in Chapter 9, but you can start by contacting the billing department or office manager in your doctor's office or the hospital to discuss the discrepancies and ask that they be fixed.

Mistake: You Don't Take Advantage of Healthcare Advocates

Healthcare advocates are experts who help patients navigate the healthcare system and fight outsized medical bills and denied claims, among other services.

The Fix: Learn What Benefits Are Available to You

If you work for a mid or large-size company, there's a good chance you have access to a host of benefits, some of which you may not be aware of, including health advocates who can help you deal with billing errors and fight denied claims, find cost estimates for medical care, get appointments with specialists, and help you understand your benefits. Ask your human resources or benefits department.

If you don't work for a company offering health advocate services, here are a number of resources you can tap into:

- Patient Advocate Foundation (www.patientadvocate.org)
- Health Proponent (www.healthproponent.com)
- MedClaims Liaison (medclaimsliaison.com)
- Medical Billing Advocates of America (billadvocates.com)

Mistake: You Don't Bother Shopping for Healthcare Prices

Imagine for a moment you're in the market for a new computer. You go into your local electronics store and choose one you like and that will suit your needs. "How much is it?" you ask the salesperson. "I don't really know," he answers.

The salesman tells you that the price of the computer depends on too many variables for him to say with certainty, right here on the spot, the full cost of the computer. So, instead, he suggests you leave a $20 deposit and take the computer home with you, and then tells you to expect a bill in the mail in a few weeks. You'll have to wait and see to learn exactly how much that bill will be.

Most people would view that scenario as ridiculous and refuse to buy the computer from that store. How would you have any way of knowing you wouldn't be charged $20,000 for the computer you've already committed to owning?

But that's just how it works in healthcare. As patients, we've been shielded from the true cost of the services we use. It's been nearly impossible to learn the true cost of our care until the bills arrive. And, as we just learned, you can't even count on the accuracy of the bills you receive.

Now that we're paying more for our healthcare, we need to understand upfront—to the extent possible—how much that care is going to cost. That requires doing some research in advance.

The Fix: Learn How to Shop for Healthcare Prices

As I discussed earlier in this chapter, the price of the same medical service can vary greatly from one doctor or hospital to another, whether you have insurance or not.

Historically, prices of medical procedures, doctor visits, and surgeries have been tough to get, but there are a lot of people working hard to make costs more transparent so that, ultimately, you can shop for the care you need like you would for any other good or service.

Insurance companies and employers are increasingly offering price comparison tools you can use for just this purpose. And the pressure on healthcare providers and health plans to make the cost of medical care more transparent is growing all the time.

Tip Check to see if your insurer or employer has a price comparison tool. It can help you save a lot of money over time.

If a cost calculator isn't available to you through your health plan or your employer, there are a number of free resources that can give you at least a ballpark figure as to what your care should cost. These tools will allow you to search for the average cost that insurance companies pay for many inpatient and outpatient procedures in your area:

- Fair Health (fairhealthconsumer.org)
- Healthcare Bluebook (healthcarebluebook.com)
- Health in Reach (healthinreach.com)
- Hospital Compare (www.hospitalcompare.hhs.gov). Among the data this tool offers are Medicare rates for a number of procedures. Add 25% to 50% to get a fair private market rate.

- New Choice Health (newchoicehealth.com)
- Cost Helper (health.costhelper.com/)

Mistake: You Don't Negotiate for the Best Price

Haggling with our doctor isn't something most of us do or even consider. But you'll increasingly be required to pay more cash out-of-pocket than before for routine doctor visits, lab tests, prescription drugs, and more. To get the best price, you need to ask for it.

The Fix: Ask for a Lower Price on Your Care

Ask your healthcare provider for the CPT (Common Procedural Terminology) code that corresponds to the service you need. Knowing the CPT code will help you find an apples-to-apples comparison, which will help you negotiate with your provider.

Enter that code into one of the online tools mentioned above. Also be sure to ask about all other services that go along with the procedure you need. For example, if you're going in for a colonoscopy, you'll want to be sure to include the cost of anesthesia and any other care you'll need. Ask for an accounting of all that's involved with the procedure.

Jargon Alert The *CPT* or *Current Procedural Terminology* is a code specific to the service or procedure your doctor will perform and that the office will use to bill for your care.

Here's a caveat: Many doctors and hospitals still can't—or won't—disclose prices up front. Bringing a print-out of the fair price you find online can help you negotiate the cost of your care.

Mistake: You Don't Ask for Care at a Less Expensive Location

As I mentioned earlier, healthcare prices vary widely from one doctor or one hospital to another. An MRI or a CT scan, drawing blood to test for the presence of diabetes, or an annual check-up—these are all standard medical services. Yet, there is a huge variation in the cost of these procedures across providers. In fact, one industry analysis found a 755% difference in the cost of the same preventive services from one doctor to another.[12] Yes, you read that right.

---

[12] Change Healthcare: Healthcare Transparency Index: www.changehealthcare.com/hcti/index.html

That means you need to do your research before going for care. And it helps to know where services are priciest so you can avoid them whenever appropriate and possible.

The Fix: Avoid Care at the Most Expensive Spots

There are a few rules of thumb when it comes to the cost of healthcare services. Hospitals, for starters, are generally the most expensive place to get care. If your doctor recommends lab tests, or imaging tests such as MRI or CT scans—even surgery—ask whether there is a cheaper spot for you to have the procedure done. Freestanding surgery centers or labs, for example, can save you a lot of money without sacrificing quality.

Beware: Some doctors' offices are actually a part of a hospital or hospital system and, because of both health reform and market forces, that's going to become more common. This means that higher hospital pricing applies. It's not always apparent, though, whether your doctor works on his or her own or is affiliated with a hospital, so here again, you'll need to ask to find out.

Locations That Can Save You Money

Retail Clinics: A fast growing and less expensive option for routine care, such as physicals, vaccines, screenings, and treatment for mild illness, is the retail clinic. Found in pharmacies and grocery stores around the country, these clinics offer convenience and low-cost care (and the prices are listed so you know exactly what you'll pay in advance!), and sometimes you can see a healthcare professional during hours when most doctors' offices are closed.[13]

Often, retail clinics are included in the insurer's network, so you may be able to use your health plan to pay for care.

Resource Alert You can find a retail clinic near you by checking the Convenient Care Association's website: www.ccaclinics.org.

Urgent Care Centers: Urgent care centers are an alternative to the emergency room. Like retail clinics, urgent care centers are popping up around the country to fill the gap between the services offered at a doctor's office and an emergency room, such as treatment for mild to moderate infections, lacerations, and bone fractures—ailments that don't pose a threat to life or limb but that need to be treated quickly by a doctor.

---

[13]Mehrotra and Lave. Visits to Retail Clinics Grew Fourfold from 2007 to 2009, Although Their Share of Overall Outpatient Visits Remain Low, *Health Affairs*: http://bit.ly/TFspax

The key here is that the price is a fraction (commonly 6 to 10 times less) of what you'll pay in the emergency department of a hospital for care that is of no lesser quality. What's more, your wait time to see a doctor is going to be significantly shorter than it would be to see someone in the ER.

Because of the convenience and lower costs, insurance companies are including these care sites in their provider networks. So even if you have health insurance, these can be a good option.

Worksite Clinics: A growing trend, especially among large employers, is to offer employees health services through a clinic based at work and staffed by nurses and doctors.

In addition to being conveniently located at or very near work, which cuts down on travel and wait times to see a healthcare provider, these sites are typically less expensive for employees.

The types of services available vary from one employer to another. Some treat sore throats, flare ups of chronic health conditions, and minor injuries. Preventive services, such as physical exams, health screenings, and immunizations are often available as well. And many offer wellness benefits such as health risk assessments, health coaching, and lifestyle management and educational programs.[14]

If your employer has an on-site clinic, it's worth looking into. Typically, the care is considerably less expensive as compared with other healthcare settings. Often employers waive co-pays or other out-of-pocket costs. Many also offer prescriptions at significantly reduced rates.

Summary

As a healthcare consumer, you've no doubt seen your costs rise over the years. There's no sign of that trend reversing.

You can't change the fact that healthcare in the United States is generally expensive. But by taking an active role in your care, and understanding how your insurance works, you can avoid many common, costly mistakes.

In the next chapter, we'll talk about how to best use your insurance benefits, as well as tips and resources for saving on another major source of healthcare costs for consumers: prescription drugs.

---

[14]Center for Studying Health System Change. Workplace Clinics, a Sign of Growing Employer Interest: www.hschange.com/CONTENT/1166/

CHAPTER 6

Buying Prescription Drugs
Tips for Saving on Medication Costs

If high prescription drug prices are eating away at your finances, you're not alone. The good news is that there are ways of keeping costs in check.

Drug Costs Are High

Each year, nearly 50 million people fail to fill their prescriptions because of costs.[1] Further, according to the Centers for Disease Control and Prevention, one out of five Americans are in families struggling to pay its medical bills, which include prescription drugs.[2]

---

[1] The Commonwealth Fund 2010 Biennial Health Insurance Survey: http://www.commonwealthfund.org/Surveys/2011/Mar/2010-Biennial-Health-Insurance-Survey.aspx

[2] Cohen, Gindi, and Kirzinger. Financial Burden of Medical Care: Early Release of Estimates from the National Health Interview Survey, January–June 2011: http://pnhp.org/blog/2012/03/07/more-on-the-financial-burden-of-medical-care/

Failure to take medications or to take them as prescribed by doctors can quickly make a health problem worse, particularly for people who have a chronic condition, such as diabetes or heart disease, that requires regular medication to manage.

What's more, part of the high cost of healthcare in the United States is attributable to what is called "prescription non-adherence"—the common occurrence of people not taking the medication prescribed to them by their doctors to improve or maintain their health.

The failure of millions of Americans to take prescribed medication is estimated to add $290 billion to this country's healthcare costs.[3] What's more, medication non-adherence is estimated to cause 125,000 deaths each year.[4]

When you consider the high cost of prescription drugs, coupled with the trend of Americans paying more out of their own pockets for medical care, it's not hard to understand why so many people are deciding to skip the pills they've been told to take.

A 2013 investigation by *Consumer Reports* magazine found that in 2012 Americans spent, on average, close to $760 each—out-of-pocket—on prescription drugs.[5]

The good news is that you can save big on many drugs by following some time-honored and newly available strategies.

Take Your Medicine

Not taking the medication prescribed to you can have an obvious negative impact on your health. But it can also cost you.

A 2011 study published in the journal *Health Affairs* found that patients with chronic illnesses who take medication as prescribed to them spend less on their overall healthcare costs than people who failed to do so.[6]

---

[3] U.S. Food and Drug Administration, Campaign to Improve Poor Medicare Adherence. Federal Register 76, no. 46, pp. 12969-12970: www.accessdata.fda.gov/scripts/oc/ohrms/dailylist.cfm?yr=2011&mn=3&dy=9

[4] American Society on Aging and the American Society of Consultant Pharmacists Foundation: www.adultmeducation.com/

[5] *Consumer Reports*, Same Generic Drug, Many Prices: www.consumerreports.org/cro/magazine/2013/05/same-generic-drug-many-prices/index.htm

[6] Roebuck, Liberman, Gemmill-Toyama, and Brennan. Medication Adherence Leads to Lower Health Care Use and Costs Despite Increased Drug Spending, *Health Affairs*: http://content.healthaffairs.org/content/30/1/91

For example, the study found that patients with congestive heart failure who stick with the medication they've been prescribed by their doctor spend $7,823 less on healthcare annually. Diabetes patients who were compliant lowered their annual healthcare costs by $3,756. And, treatment for hypertension costs $3,908 less per patient per year for people who take their prescribed medication.

The cost savings were even greater for people age 65 and older, according to the research.

Bottom line: Taking medications necessary to manage illness can be critical to both your health and your wallet.

Talk with Your Doctor and Pharmacist

Although taking medications as they're prescribed is important, that doesn't mean you should agree blindly to pop all pills suggested to you without getting more information.

One of the most important things you can do is question both your doctor and your pharmacist about prescription costs. If you're finding it hard to afford your medication, it's important to let them know. Often, there are less costly, equally effective alternatives available.

For example, generics, compared with brand-name drugs, can make a huge difference in how much you spend on medication. Many prescription drugs are available in generic form and cost significantly less than the name-brand version. If a generic isn't offered to you, ask your physician if one is available.

Another conversation you want to have with your doctor is whether the drug being prescribed is one you really need to take.

"Many times medicines get prescribed when they are not needed," said Richard Sagall, M.D. president of NeedyMeds, a website offering information about financial assistance to pay for medication (www.needymeds.org). Here are a few questions Dr. Sagall suggests you ask your doctor:

- How is this going to affect my condition?
- What happens if I don't take it?
- How is this going to change my treatment?

Know Thy Formulary

Formulary—health insurer-speak for "list of medicines"—refers to the drugs that a particular health plan does and does not pay for. The list can vary widely from carrier to carrier and even from year to year within a single plan. So you can't assume that a drug that was covered last year will be covered next year.

Chapter 6 | Buying Prescription Drugs

> **Jargon Alert** You'll hear the word *formulary* quite a bit when you talk to insurers or access health plan documents. It simply refers to a list of the particular drugs a plan will pay for.

Drugs are organized into tiers, with different co-pays. Tier 1 has the lowest co-pay or no co-pay at all, and it usually includes generic drugs. Tier 2 has a higher co-pay, and generally includes widely prescribed, non-generic drugs. Tier 3 drugs—often newer or less prescribed medications—have higher co-pays because they cost the insurer more.

The formulary for your policy can usually be found on your insurance company's website or you can get it by calling your insurer. Showing it to your doctor could help him or her choose medications that are covered by your insurer, which may save you money.

Also common is a process called "step therapy" in which your insurer requires you to try a number of less expensive drugs before agreeing to cover a more costly brand-name medication. In some cases the quantity of the medication you can buy is limited; your insurer may want confirmation that it's working before agreeing to cover the next prescription.

COST ALERT!

Keep in mind that just because a drug is covered under your insurance plan, it doesn't mean your co-pay is the best deal you can get.

Believe it or not, the retail price of certain drugs may actually be lower at some pharmacies than many insurance co-pays. This is especially true for widely prescribed, generic drugs. It may pay to ask your pharmacist the retail price of a drug before handing over your insurance card.

A *Consumer Reports* investigation found that big discount stores like Costco, in addition to drugstore websites, and a few independent pharmacies had retail prices that were lower for certain drugs than many insurance co-pays.[7]

It Pays to Shop Around

Whether you are paying for your prescription drugs out-of-pocket or have a co-pay, shopping around can save you money.

A recent investigation by *Consumer Reports* magazine showed huge variations in the cost of popular prescription drugs.

---

[7]*Consumer Reports*, Same Generic Drug, Many Prices: www.consumerreports.org/cro/magazine/2013/05/same-generic-drug-many-prices/index.htm

Calls were made to 200 pharmacies throughout the U.S. to get prices on a month's supply of five blockbuster medications now available as generics: the diabetes drug Actos (pioglitazone), the antidepressant Lexapro (escitalopram), the statin Lipitor (atorvastatin), the blood thinner Plavix (clopidogrel), and the asthma drug Singulair (montelukast).

The investigation revealed a startling $749, or 447%, difference between the costs of the five drugs at different vendors.

The big-box giant Costco had the lowest prices of the merchants contacted, with a 30-day supply of all five prescriptions costing just $167, while the pharmacy CVS was the most expensive, with the five prescriptions costing $916.

Several online pharmacies, including Healthwarehouse.com and FamilyMeds.com, had some of the lowest prices, with the five prescriptions averaging around $200. Target and Rite Aid were among the most expensive, with the average closer to $800.

Costco consistently beat the chain drugstores and even online sellers on price in the *Consumer Reports* investigation, and a Costco membership is not required to use the pharmacy.

Ask for the Best Price

The same *Consumer Reports* study found that in many cases, callers were quoted a higher price on the drugs they requested unless they specifically asked for the lowest price.

Here's the simplest piece of advice you'll ever get about saving money on your prescription drugs: Ask the pharmacy for the best price.

And don't forget to ask about special promotions you might be eligible for, like senior, student or membership discounts.

Tip Are you getting the lowest possible price for your prescription? Maybe or maybe not, so simply ask: "Is this the lowest price you offer on this drug?"

Saving with Medicare Part D

The Affordable Care Act includes provisions to make prescription drugs less expensive for Medicare recipients by closing the Medicare Part D prescription drug coverage gap, commonly known as the "donut hole."

Under the healthcare law, people covered by Part D who enter the donut hole now receive more than a 50% discount on name brand drugs and 14% for generics.[8]

Coverage will increase over the next several years. By 2020 recipients will pay just 25% of the cost of brand-name and generic prescription drugs in the coverage gap.

According to U.S. Department of Health and Human Services, more than 6 million seniors and people with disabilities have saved over $6.1 billion on prescription drugs since the Affordable Care Act became law in 2010.[9]

In 2012 alone, 3.5 million Medicare recipients saved an average of around $706 each as a result of the closing of the donut hole coverage gap.

Get Extra Help

Medicare Extra Help is a Medicare program that offers assistance to pay for premiums for Part D prescription drug coverage, the Medicare drug benefit program. The program has income and asset limits.

This program includes single people with annual incomes (in 2013) below $17,235 or married couples with an annual income of $23,265. In addition, to qualify, an individual cannot have assets worth more than $13,300; married couples living together are limited to resources amounting to $26,560 or less. Homes, cars, and personal possessions do not count as resources.[10]

You can learn if you qualify by doing a self-screening online at benefitscheckup.org, a service of the National Council on Aging.

Resource Alert To enroll in Medicare Extra Help, call the Social Security Administration at 800-772-1213. You can also connect online at www.ssa.gov or visit your local Social Security office.

---

[8]Medicare Rights Center. Closing the Donut Hole: www.medicarerights.org/pdf/Closing-the-Doughnut-Hole-Chart.pdf
[9]Medicare.gov. The Medicare Blog: Nearly 3.5 million saved more than $706 on prescriptions: http://blog.medicare.gov/2013/03/25/nearly-3-5-million-people-saved-more-than-706-on-prescriptions-in-2012/
[10]Social Security: www.ssa.gov/pubs/media/pdf/EN-05-10525.pdf

Try a Discount Drug Card

Discount drug cards are pretty much what their name suggests: They offer discounts on prescription medications as well as over-the-counter drugs, medical supplies, and even pet prescription drugs.

These are not insurance cards; in fact, you cannot use these cards along with your insurance. They are offered by state governments, drug companies, and non-profit and for-profit businesses.[11]

These cards can, in some cases, save you as much as 80–85% off the cash price of medications. However, the savings available vary greatly, and there are a few pitfalls to watch for when selecting the right card:[12]

1. Never pay for one of these cards. There are many good, free discount cards available.

2. Do not register a discount drug card. When you register your card, the card marketer gains access to useful marketing information about you that it can sell.

3. Verify that the card marketer does not market the information it has about the transactions. Marketers can get all sorts of information about every transaction their card is used for, including a patient's name and address. Some people will sell that information.

Download an App or Two

A high-tech way to search for savings is by using one of the increasing number of apps that promise to slash your drug bills.

Most compare drug prices among area pharmacies and they claim savings as high as 85%.

Some of the most popular include:

- **GoodRX.** This free app compares prices at local and online pharmacies and offers coupons and savings tips available on your smartphone. It also sends reminders when it's time to refill prescriptions with current prices at area pharmacies (www.goodrx.com).

---

[11]NeedyMeds.org. Drug Discount Cards: www.needymeds.org/indices/discountcards.htm
[12]Author's conversation with Dr. Richard Sagall, NeedyMeds.org

- **LowestMed.** Also free, LowestMed is a discount prescription program. It also compares prices, but users must present a free discount card when they pick up their prescriptions to get the quoted price (www.lowestmed.com).
- **Prescription Saver.** Prescription Saver promises to save users up to 75% off of brand-name and generic prescription drugs. The app also helps you find the pharmacy and lets you save those you use to your favorites.

Also, the pharmacy chains Walgreens, CVS, and Rite Aid have all launched their own free apps to help customers organize their prescriptions and search for savings.

All promise to make it easier for customers to refill prescriptions, manage their customer loyalty programs, and download photos to be developed.

Walgreens' app also includes discount coupons, and it will even remind users when it's time to take their medicine.

Check Out the Web

Buying prescription drugs online is often less expensive than getting them from your neighborhood pharmacy.

Consumer Reports found that shopping online for drugs can save consumers 35% or more off the retail price of their medicines.[13]

It's important to look for websites verified by the National Association of Boards of Pharmacy (http://www.nabp.net/), which issues a Verified Internet Pharmacy Practices Site (VIPPS) to websites that have been vetted. There are many online pharmacies that aren't legitimate, so this is a good source to confirm that you're buying from a reputable vendor.

Some well-known sites with the VIPPS seal include:
- Drugstores.com
- Familymeds.com
- Walgreens.com
- CVS.com
- Costco.com

---

[13]*Consumer Reports.* Comparison Shopping, Getting the Best Price on Your Drugs: www.consumerreports.org/health/resources/pdf/best-buy-drugs/money-saving-guides/english/BestPrice-FINAL.pdf

> **Tip** When buying drugs online, be sure the vendor is legitimate. Look for the VIPPS seal of approval.

Save Bucks with Buying Clubs

An increasing number of retailers offer generic prescriptions to their customers at rock-bottom prices.

Walmart started the trend in October 2006, introducing its "$4 Prescription Program" for a 30-day supply on hundreds of generic drugs and over-the-counter medications. The popular plan was quickly copied by other chains, including Target.

A 2011 study found that even though the programs save people in the U.S. billions of dollars a year, they could be saving much more. Millions of people who could be saving money through the programs were not taking advantage of them.[14]

Although the $4 prescription programs are intended for everyone, Walgreens, CVS, and Rite Aid pharmacies all also offer prescription savings programs intended for people who are uninsured or can't afford their medications even with health insurance.

Descriptions of the programs can be found on the chains' websites listed in the previous section.

Split the Difference

Pill splitting—literally cutting medications in half—is a long-used strategy for saving money on many drugs. Because dosage is often not a factor in a drug's price, asking your doctor to prescribe a drug in double the dosage you need and then cutting the pill in half can yield two doses of medication for the price of one.

Many drugs can be split safely, but it is never a good idea to split pills unless your doctor agrees.

Splitting pills should be done carefully and with the right tools. Never use a knife, which can be both dangerous and imprecise. Pill splitters, which do the job neatly, can be purchased inexpensively from any pharmacy.

---

[14]Zhang. Potential Savings from Greater Use of $4 Generic Drugs. *Arch Internal Medicine*: www.ncbi.nlm.nih.gov/pmc/articles/PMC3074338/

Chapter 6 | Buying Prescription Drugs

SAFETY ALERT!

Pill splitting—buying double the dosage and cutting the pill in half—can save you money. But some drugs cannot be split. These include time-released medications and capsules and many other drugs such as:

- Anti-seizure drugs
- Birth control pills
- Blood thinners such as Coumadin and warfarin
- Chemotherapy drugs
- Pills with hard outside coatings

The easiest pills to split have scored centers, but you should not assume it's safe to split every pill that is scored. Also, pills should be split only in half, not in quarters.

Websites That Can Help

There are countless public and private assistance programs available to help people pay for their prescription drugs if they can't afford them, but educating yourself about the available options can be daunting.

Groups that can help include RxAssist (www.rxassist.org), NeedyMeds (www.needymeds.org), and Partnership for Prescription Assistance (www.pparx.org). All three organizations have websites that serve as information clearinghouses for a wide range of drug assistance programs, as well as programs that will help you fill out the applications needed to apply.

Some states, including New York, Michigan, and Florida, also have websites that help consumers compare drug prices at in-state pharmacies. Check with your state's department of insurance for more information.

One more good source for tips on how to save money on drugs is the *Consumer Reports* Best Buy Drugs webpage (consumerreports.org).

Additional Cost Saving Tips

Just about anyone can save money on their prescription drugs, but it may take a little work.

Some final thoughts and novel strategies:

- **You gotta ask.** Remember, if you want the best price on a drug you need to ask for it.

- **Compare your co-pay.** Make sure your co-pay isn't costing you more than if you simply bought the drug outright. Be sure to ask your pharmacist if the retail price of the drug is less than the price of your co-pay.

- **Think generic.** Many widely prescribed drugs have recently become available as generics, or will be available soon, meaning big savings for patients. Be sure to ask your doctor if the medication you need is available in generic form.

- **Refill prescriptions for 90 days.** Many drug retailers offer discounts on a three-month supply, compared to a one-month supply. It is not a good idea to do this with new drug prescriptions, though, unless you are sure you will stay on the medication and your doctor will not change your dosage.

- **Get out of town.** If you live in an urban area, you might find lower prices on your drugs at suburban or rural pharmacies. *Consumer Reports* found that a month-supply of the generic version of Actos cost $203 at an independent pharmacy in the city of Raleigh, North Carolina, while a pharmacy in a more rural area of the state charged $37.

- **Go online or go "big box."** When it comes to prescription drug prices, big-box retailers such as Costco and Sam's Club, and reputable online pharmacies, tend to beat the independent and chain pharmacies. They don't offer the full range of services that many traditional chain and independent drugstores do, though. So if price is not your main consideration, they may not be for you.

- **Review your meds often.** Especially if you take a lot of drugs, it is important to review the medications on a regular basis with your doctor or doctors. You may find that you no longer need to be on certain drugs, or that you can substitute a similar, less expensive drug for a costlier one.

- **Join a clinical trial.** If you have chronic or other serious illnesses and cannot get insurance to pay for an experimental or "off-label" use of a drug, consider signing up for a clinical trial. This is a great way to get excellent health care at no or very low cost. Search `ClinicalTrials.gov`, a clearinghouse maintained by the National Institutes of Health.

Summary

Greater use of generic drugs has helped to lower the overall cost of prescription drugs in recent years. Still, the expense of medication is often a barrier for people who need treatments to improve or maintain the state of their health.

By understanding where and how to find the best prices on prescription drugs, you can save yourself a lot of money.

In the next chapter we'll talk about additional ways to lower your costs by knowing your rights and how to fight back when medical billing mistakes occur, or you're denied access to benefits to which you believe you're entitled.

CHAPTER 7

You Against the Healthcare System
Finding and Fighting Billing Errors

Medical billing mistakes are far more common than most people realize. Knowing where to look for errors and how to fight back can make a huge difference in the cost of your medical care.

Don't Be Fooled

Americans love a bargain.

For some people, shopping around for a great deal on everything from a new car to a can of soup is a way of life, and comparing prices is in their DNA.

Yet it's a safe bet that most dedicated bargain hunters don't know much about healthcare costs. And, if you read Chapter 5 of this book, you now understand how healthcare prices are created in a way that bears little connection to the actual cost of providing care. Prices, in fact, vary greatly depending on whether or not you have insurance, the type of insurance you have, and which healthcare provider delivers your care. The saying "You get what you pay for" does not apply in healthcare. In fact, studies have repeatedly shown that the price of a medical service or procedure has no relationship to the quality of healthcare you'll receive.

Historically, we've also had very little incentive to pay close attention to the cost of care or what's being charged. For most of us, health insurance has covered a big chunk of our medical bills. We had no need to examine the cost closely or question whether or not it was fair and reasonable.

That's rapidly changing. Increasingly, we're on the hook for a larger amount of the cost of the medical care we get. That means paying close attention to where you go for care and what you're charged will grow in importance.

Still, few people shop for healthcare or even recognize when they are paying too much, even though medical costs may be some of the biggest expenses families face whether they have health insurance or not.

And when medical billing errors occur, even fewer people know how to spot them and what actions to take to address overcharges.

As a result, in the United States we pay billions more than we should each year for healthcare.

Medical Billing Advocates of America—a company that goes to bat for consumers to dispute erroneous medical charges—says 80% of the hospital bills it reviews contain errors. And those errors usually favor the healthcare provider.[1]

Insurance companies commonly make claims processing mistakes as well, although the industry's record has improved in recent years. According to the American Medical Association's National Health Insurer Report Card, commercial health insurers have a claims processing error rate of 7.1% in 2013, down from 20% in 2010.[2]

And, by one estimate, as much as 3% of all healthcare spending—tens of billions of dollars a year—is lost to deliberate overcharging and fraud.

Common Pitfalls That Will Cost You

It shouldn't be this way, but the fact is that medical billing is highly confusing and often riddled with mistakes. That means you should approach each bill with some skepticism.

---

[1] Medical Billing Advocates of America: www.billadvocates.com/images/stories/pdfs/Medical%20Bill%20Survival%20Guide.pdf
[2] American Medical Association 2013 National Health Insurer Report Card: www.ama-assn.org/resources/doc/psa/2013-nhirc-comparison.pdf

As I discussed in Chapter 5, some of the most common billing errors—especially during hospital stays—include:

- Billing for more hospital days than you stayed
- Billing for more time in the operating room than was used
- Double billing for medical procedures, supplies, services, or medications
- Excessive charges ($16 for one pill of Tylenol, anyone?)
- Charges for doctor visits or tests you never got
- Miscoded medical procedures and services
- Being billed for non-billable items, such as gloves, drapes, sutures, cotton balls, and tissues. These items are included in the price of your hospital room and should never be billed separately.
- Being billed full price for treatment by out-of-network doctors you didn't agree to see

Following are some pitfalls to avoid and how to take action if you find yourself in one of these situations.

Pitfall: You Don't Review All Bills and Statements

As mentioned at the start of this chapter, there is a better-than-even chance that a medical bill contains errors, so if you pay bills without reviewing them carefully, there's also a good chance you or your insurer is paying more than necessary.

The Fix: Read Everything That Crosses Your Desk

Be vigilant about checking to see if you were billed for the right number of hospital days after a hospital stay, and look for duplicate or excessive charges for tests or other services and for services you never got. If the bill is for a procedure provided in your doctor's office, make sure the charges coincide with what you know took place.

Contact your physician's office manager or the billing department of the hospital where you received care right away if you suspect errors.

Pitfall: You Don't Ask for an Itemized Bill

To do the best possible job reviewing your bills, you need to know exactly what the charges comprise. Yet, more often than not, the bill sent to you by your healthcare provider is a summary bill. Rather than showing you an itemized accounting of all the services that make up the bill's contents, it gives you a listing of charges by category. For example, you'll likely see a charge for your room, another for pharmacy, and yet another for laboratory and medical supplies. Without listing each item individually, however, it's easy for the provider to bury costs you shouldn't be paying for.

Pat Palmer, founder of Medical Billing Advocates of America, points out in her book: *The Medical Bill Survival Guide: What you Need to Know Before You Pay a Dime*, that the summary bill is analogous to a receipt from the grocery store that looks something like this:

Produce: $31.66
Dairy: $18.07
Toiletries: $25.81[3]

What did you actually buy? Unless you receive a bill that lists each medical service, item, and medication delivered, you won't know.

The Fix: Demand an Itemized Bill

Sadly, it's not uncommon for patients to meet with resistance when requesting an itemized bill. Providers—hospitals in particular—know that if you're able to view each and every detail, they're liable to have some explaining to do.

Contact the billing department at either the hospital or medical group where you received services. Let them know that you want an itemized bill. If they give you a hard time, tell you they can't give it to you, or you should have asked for it before leaving the hospital, for example, let them know you are aware of your legal rights to have it, and that they are required by law to give you an itemized bill.

If you still get the run-around, move your way up the ladder of the organization. You can start by contacting the director of billing. If you don't get satisfaction there go to the hospital's chief financial officer or even chief executive officer by sending a written letter by certified mail.

Review the itemized bill line by line. If there's something out of order, you have the right to dispute or question the charges.

---

[3] Pat Palmer, *The Medical Bill Survival Guide, What You Need to Know Before You Pay a Dime*: www.amazon.com/Medical-Bill-Survival-Guide-Revised/dp/061556044X/

Pitfall: You Don't Know What Your Insurer Paid

Billing errors often occur when doctors or hospitals improperly bill your insurer. This is especially common when you have more than one type of insurance. There may be confusion about which insurer should pay first and which one should pay the balance. Or, it may simply be that your healthcare provider billed for something he or she should not have, or coded the service improperly.

The Fix: Wait for Your Explanation of Benefits

Before you pay medical charges, you need to make sure your insurer(s) has(ve) been billed and paid the proper amount.

The key to doing this is by waiting for and then carefully reviewing the Explanation of Benefits (EOB).

If you have health insurance, the first document you receive after a doctor visit, a stay in the hospital, or a medical procedure is likely to be your EOB.[4] EOBs are the documents sent to you by your health plan explaining what your provider charged your insurer and how much of that amount your policy will cover. They tend to look just like bills, but they're not. In fact, you'll see the words "This is not a bill" printed somewhere on the page.

Jargon Alert An "Explanation of Benefits," or EOB, shows what your healthcare provider billed your insurance company and how much your insurer will pay. You will receive this soon after receiving care.

EOBs don't all look alike, but they all should contain the same basic information, including:

- Your insurance ID number and claim number
- A numerical code or codes for the health services you received. These are called common procedural terminology codes (CPTs).
- A brief description of the service and the date that it was performed
- The amount the provider billed, which may show up on the form as "submitted charges"

---

[4]See this sample EOB from Cigna: www.cigna.com/assets/docs/explanation-of-benefits/explanationOfBenefits832700.pdf

- The amount your insurer paid for the service, which is often called the "negotiated" or "allowed amount"
- How much of the amount left unpaid by your insurer you owe to your provider, and if you have an obligation to pay your provider with co-payments or deductibles

BEFORE YOU PAY THAT BILL...

Don't pay any medical bills until you've received your EOB and had a chance to review it carefully. You want to compare the services you received against what the EOB says your provider billed your insurer.

Check to make sure the CPT codes—the 5-digit code assigned to every medical service and procedure providers use to bill insurers—are the same on the bill your provider sent you as those listed on the EOB. If they don't match, call both your provider and your insurer to get to the bottom of the discrepancy.

Pitfall: You Don't Get the Negotiated Rate

Even if you haven't yet met your plan's deductible and are paying for 100% of your care, you are entitled to receive the discounted rate your insurer has negotiated with your healthcare provider. When a healthcare provider (doctor, hospital, lab, etc.) is contracted with your insurance company, it's considered in-network and has agreed to accept a discounted rate from your insurer. You are entitled to be billed at that same rate, which will be significantly lower than what the provider would otherwise charge.

Yet, it's not uncommon for insurance companies to process the claim without applying the discount, leaving you on the hook for a higher sum.

The Fix: Demand the In-Network Rate

Your first step is to confirm that you were charged the rate your insurer has negotiated with the provider, which you can do by calling your insurer and asking.

This is another reason why reviewing your EOB is so important. If the amount showing what your provider billed your insurer is the same as the amount listed as "allowed charges," there's a good chance you didn't get the discount to which you're entitled. Ask your insurer to re-process the claim.

Pitfall: You Don't Shop for the Best Price

As discussed in Chapter 5, with many of us now paying more of our healthcare expenses, it's more important than ever to understand how much that care is going to cost. Naturally, if you're facing a life-threatening illness or injury, you're not going to take the time to compare prices before seeking medical help. But for non-urgent or elective medical care, you need to remember that prices vary widely, even within the same insurance company network of providers. Therefore, comparing prices is always in your best financial interest.

The Fix: Learn How to Shop for Healthcare Prices

It's still not easy to nail down a firm price for medical procedures. But healthcare providers are under growing pressure from employers, the government, the public, and others to make their prices available.

Insurance companies and employers are increasingly offering price comparison tools you can use for just this purpose. And a number of large employers have begun to contract with hospitals and other healthcare providers willing to provide workers major medical services, such as surgeries, for one negotiated lump sum fee.

As discussed in Chapter 5, there are also free resources available for you to use when trying to understand what your care should cost. These tools will allow you to search for the average cost that insurance companies pay for many inpatient and outpatient procedures in your area:

- Fair Health (fairhealthconsumer.org)
- Healthcare Bluebook (healthcarebluebook.com)
- Health in Reach (healthinreach.com)
- New Choice Health (newchoicehealth.com)
- Cost Helper (health.costhelper.com)

Pitfall: You Don't Negotiate for the Best Price

Haggling with your doctor isn't something most of us do or even consider. But you'll increasingly be required to pay more cash out-of-pocket than before for routine doctor visits, lab tests, prescription drugs, and more. To get the best price, you need to ask for it.

The Fix: Ask for a Discount

Ask your healthcare provider for the CPT (Common Procedural Terminology) code that corresponds to the service you need.

Enter that code into one of the online tools mentioned earlier. Also be sure to ask about all other services that go along with the procedure you need. For example, if you're going in for a colonoscopy, you'll want to be sure to include the cost of anesthesia and any other care you'll need. Ask for an accounting of all that's involved with the procedure.

■ **Tip** You're likely to get some push back from healthcare providers who say they can't or won't give you a firm price up front. Bring a printout of the fair price you find online through one of the pricing websites. Tell your doctor/hospital, "This is what I know to be a fair price in this area for this service. This is what I'm willing to pay." That will at least start the process of negotiation.

Many doctors and hospitals still can't—or won't—disclose prices up front. Bringing a printout of the fair price you find online can help you negotiate the cost of your care.

This is particularly important if you don't have health insurance or have a very high deductible that might require you to pay thousands of dollars before your insurance kicks in.

In his 2013 book examining the American healthcare system, *Catastrophic Care*, Game Show Network president David Goldhill tells the story of shopping around for a magnetic resonance imaging (MRI) scan when his sister-in-law suffered a knee injury while visiting from Russia.

Because she was not a U.S. citizen and did not have insurance, she faced paying the full cost of the diagnostic imaging test out of pocket.

The initial price of the MRI, quoted by their physician's usual provider, was $1500. When Goldhill's wife started making calls to other MRI providers—making sure to share the previous best price with each one—the cost dropped quickly, first to $1200, then $800, and then $650.

"Finally, one specialist said he would take $300, but only if payment was by check (not credit card) and only if we could show up at four o'clock the next day," Goldhill wrote. "When I tell friends the story of our MRI price shopping, I get an almost identical reaction: 'You can do that? Doctors will negotiate price with you?' "[5]

---

[5]Goldhill, David. *Catastrophic Care: How American Health Care Killed My Father—and How We Can Fix It.* New York: Alfred A. Knopf, 2013, p. 64

Pitfall: You Fall Prey to Balance Billing

Balance billing describes a practice by healthcare providers in which they go after you for money you don't owe.

Typically, the doctor or hospital is contracted with your insurance company. The provider in this case charges you the difference between what the health plan pays and what the provider feels he or she (or the hospital) is owed.

Most states have laws against balance billing; doctors, other healthcare providers, and hospitals that contract with a health plan must accept the rate they have agreed to. It's also illegal for all Medicare services.

If a healthcare provider is in your health insurer's network, it cannot charge you more than the cost of your deductibles, co-pays, or co-insurance. This doesn't apply, however, when a doctor or hospital does not participate with your insurer.

The Fix: Take Steps to Avoid It and Then Fight Back

There are several strategies to reduce the risk of balance billing.

Stay in network. You limit your risk of errant billing and increase your chances of getting help from your insurer if you get care from healthcare providers who participate in your insurer's provider network. Once you go out of the network, your insurer no longer has a contract to which it can hold the provider responsible.

Know your plan. Be clear in advance of going for care (whenever possible) what services and benefits are covered by your insurer.

Know the law. Make sure you know your state's laws regarding balance billing. Check with your state's department of insurance.

Call the provider out. Confirm your insurer's policy on balance billing. Once you have this information in hand, along with the knowledge of your state's laws about balance billing, contact the doctor or hospital that sent the bill. Let them know what they're doing is considered balance billing and that's it's not a legitimate practice, and that you want the bill eliminated.

Contact your insurer. If you're unsuccessful with your provider, get your insurance company involved. After all, the relationship is between your insurer and your provider, and the insurer has a responsibility to ensure the doctor or hospital is complying with its contract.

Go further. If you meet with resistance from both your provider and your insurer, you can file a complaint with your state's department of insurance and/or the attorney general's office.

Resolving Medical Billing Disputes

After receiving medical care, particularly after a hospital stay, it's a fair bet you can expect an onslaught of medical bills. Some may even be from providers you've never heard of or for services you didn't know you received.

Sometimes a simple phone call to the medical group or hospital can clear things up. Unfortunately, however, more often than not you'll have to go further. When you run into trouble with medical bills, here are the steps you want to take.

1. **Put it in writing.** All communication you have with a healthcare provider about billing disputes should be put in writing. Clearly outline each item you're challenging. Request the removal of inaccurate charges or a written response with documentation to support the charges.

2. **Kick it up the chain.** If you're unsuccessful in your initial dealing with staff in the billing department, don't waste any more of your time. As mentioned earlier in this chapter, you should go to the top of the organization's food chain. Write another letter addressed to the chief financial officer or chief executive officer of the hospital or medical group where you received care. Again, outline your billing concerns and make it clear that you have tried and failed to settle the matter with the billing department. Be sure to send the letter by certified mail. And always keep copies of all correspondence, including bills and canceled checks. Also keep a record of the name and number of anyone you speak with. This will be especially helpful if you have to take your case outside the hospital.

3. **Call your insurance company**. If you have health insurance, get your insurance company involved. Particularly if the providers you saw are in your insurer's network, the company has a responsibility to assist you.

4. **Ask your doctor for help.** If you have a good relationship with your doctor, mention that you're having trouble with a bill that was produced by his or her office. If the medical bill stems from a hospital stay and your physician has admitting privileges at that hospital, he or she may be willing to advocate on your behalf.

5. **Negotiate.** As discussed in chapter 5, do some homework by checking with your insurer or through websites such as www.Fairhealth.org for a fair price for the care you received. Use that as a starting point to negotiate with the provider. If you can pay cash, your chances of knocking down the price are even better. If your account has already been sent to collections, your credit is going to take a hit, so you want to avoid this scenario whenever possible. However, once it's happened, it's worth an attempt to negotiate to lower how much of the bill you'll pay.

6. **Put it on hold.** If you're disputing charges, notify the medical group or hospital in writing that your account should be placed on hold until the dispute is resolved, and that it not be sent to collections.

7. **Know your rights.** If you don't have insurance it is important to know that a few states now limit how much hospitals can charge patients who are footing the bill for their own care. Check with your state's department of insurance to learn about the laws where you live.

8. **File a complaint.** If you are being stonewalled by your provider, file a complaint with your state's department of public health or insurance. You can also contact your state's attorney general's office for assistance. To find contact information for your state's department of insurance, go to the website for the National Association of Insurance Commissioners (www.naic.org) and click on the tab that says "States and Jurisdiction Map."

Fighting Denied Insurance Claims

It is a big mistake to assume that being denied coverage by your insurance company means the decision about whether or not your care will be paid for is final.

In fact, a 2011 report by the Government Accountability Office (GAO) found that in some parts of the country, in nearly 6 in 10 health insurance appeals in which a patient fought a denial of coverage, the insurer reversed its original decision.[6]

---

[6] U.S. Government Accountability Office. Private Health Insurance Data on Application and Coverage Denials: www.gao.gov/products/GAO-11-268

Bottom line: It's well worth your time to fight a denied claim. And, as I discuss in earlier chapters, the Affordable Care Act has expanded consumers' right to appeal. You're entitled to both an internal appeal (conducted by your insurer) and an external appeal (conducted by a third party) if your insurer rules against you.

There are a number of common reasons why your claim might have been denied.

Your Provider Isn't in the Network

You were treated at a hospital or by a doctor who is not in your health plan's network. Typically, you are reimbursed a considerably lower amount for care you receive with an out-of-network provider than you would for a provider contracted with your insurer. And, in some cases—for example, if you are covered by an HMO—you're insurer won't cover the cost of out-of-network services at all.

The Service Is Not a Covered Benefit

Before seeking services, it's imperative that you check with your insurer to make sure the care you need is a covered benefit.

You Didn't Get the Go-Ahead

Often, insurers require that you gain prior approval or "pre-authorization" before you receive a medical service or procedure. Without prior approval, your care or prescription for medications can be denied. When it comes to prescription drugs, your insurer may use something called "step therapy." In that case, you'll be required to first try an alternative—typically a generic drug—before your insurer will pay for certain medications prescribed by your doctor.

Billing Errors

Sometimes providers make mistakes when billing an insurance company. It could be that important information or codes are missing, or something was billed incorrectly. In this case, the mistake simply needs to be corrected and the bill resubmitted.

By understanding the details of your health plan and any rules you are required to follow, you can minimize denials.

Filing Your Complaint

The health reform law gives most consumers the right to challenge their health plan's decisions. (So-called "grandfathered" health plans, which were already in place when the act became law on March 23, 2010, are exempt from complying.)

By law, your health plan has to send you instructions about how to initiate an appeal when it denies payment and spell out any deadlines for filing it. The notices from your insurer should also include information about how to contact your state's Consumer Assistance Program (if there is one in your state), which can help with insurance disputes. (See the Appendix for contact information for Consumer Assistance Programs and departments of insurance around the country.)

You have the right to appeal your insurer's decision if your plan tells you:

- The care for which you're requesting coverage is not medically necessary.
- You are not eligible for the health plan or benefit.
- Your care isn't covered because your plan says you have a pre-existing health condition.
- The medical care you want is experimental.[7]

The Internal Appeal

Your first step is what's called an internal appeal. This is the process through which your health plan reviews its decision to deny payment. Although the appeal process is with your health plan, the people doing the actual review must be different from those who made the original determination.

You have the right to understand details behind your insurer's decision to deny. That includes getting access to the plan's file about your case and the medical decision-making process behind the denial.

If your care was denied because it's being viewed as experimental, you should ask for your doctor's support in providing medical justification for the treatment. You can also collect your own medical support by searching for journal articles on PubMed, a service of the U.S. National Library of Medicine, at www.pubmed.gov.

---

[7] FamiliesUSA.org: Your Right to Appeal: www.familiesusa.org/health-reform-central/september-23/Your-Right-to-Appeal.pdf

You also have the right to request help from your state's Consumer Assistance Program to settle disputes over coverage and billing. Further, you can request that your insurer keep paying your medical bills until the dispute is settled.[8]

After you file an internal appeal, the insurer has 72 hours after receiving your request to rule on the appeal if you are denied a claim for urgent care and 30 days if the denial is for non-urgent care if that care has not yet been given.

When non-urgent care has already been provided, the insurer has 60 days to rule.

If you get your health benefits at work, particularly if you work for a large company, it's likely that your employer pays its own medical claims. In this case, a service not covered by your health plan is best discussed with your company's benefits department. Depending on the issue, they may be willing to cover the cost of the medical service you need.

External Appeals

If you're unsatisfied with the outcome of your insurer's internal appeal, you can initiate what's called an external appeal. Your case will be reviewed by doctors who do not work with your health plan.

In many places, this is handled by the state's department of insurance; sometimes an independent review organization conducts external reviews. You can contact the department of insurance in your state for assistance.

Employer-funded health plans (most health plans offered by large employers) are enforced by the U.S. Department of Labor: You can contact them by calling (866) 444-3272 or by going to their website, www.askebsa.dol.gov.

Calling in the Experts: Getting Help with Billing Disputes

There are a number of resources available when you need help dealing with your medical bills.

- Many states have Consumer Assistance Programs (CAPs), which offer help to consumers with health insurance problems. You can find a program in your state at Healthcare.gov. The Appendix also provides a list of CAPs and departments of insurance by state.

- The nonprofit Patient Advocate Foundation (www.patientadvocate.org) offers help appealing health insurance decisions free of charge.

---

[8]Ibid.

- There are a number of companies that provide services that help consumers find billing errors and make sense of opaque medical bills. They will also negotiate with the insurer or provider for you when you dispute a bill:
    - Claims.org
    - Hospitalbillreview.com
    - Healthproponent.com
    - Billadvocates.com
    - Healthchampion.net
    - Patientcare4u.com

Many large and even mid-sized companies now offer medical billing advocacy services to their employees as part of their health benefits packages. These services might include helping you make sense of your bills and disputing suspected inaccuracies.

Check with your company's benefits department to learn if this service is available to you.

Getting Hold of Your Medical Records

There are many reasons to gain access to your medical records. When it comes to fighting medical bills, your records can be useful in helping to determine what services you received while in the hospital or play a role in fighting a denial of coverage that was decided on the basis of medical need.

One of the most common complaints I hear is how difficult it is for people to get their records. Here's what you need to know.

- **It's your right.** Both federal and often state law protect your right to view and get a copy of your medical records.
- **Put it in writing.** In most cases, you'll need to put your request to either see or gain a copy of your medical records in writing. It's always a good idea to send the request by certified mail so that you have a record of it having been received.
- **You may have to pay.** Doctors and hospitals are allowed by law to charge a reasonable fee to make the copies of your records. You cannot be charged, however, for reviewing them. Rates vary by state. To learn what the rules are where you live go to the website for

Georgetown University's Center on Medical Record Rights and Privacy at: http://medicalrecordrights.georgetown.edu/records.html. You can also request that your doctor provide you with a summary of your records. For this service, you can also be charged a fee.

- **Time limits apply.** Your healthcare provider is required to respond to your request in a timely manner, although the timelines vary by state. In some states your request to view your medical records has to be granted within 5 business days, for example. However, your doctor can withhold the records until you pay the required fees.

- **You can ask for help.** If you run into trouble getting your records, look first to your state medical board for help. There's a link to all state medical boards at the American Medical Association website (www.ama-assn.org), under the education and careers tab. Complaints can also be filed with the Department of Health and Human Services Office for Civil Rights (www.hhs.gov/ocr).

Summary

Medical bills are a very confusing aspect of the healthcare system, and unfortunately, a big cause of bankruptcy in this country.

The Affordable Care Act puts protections in place with new options for consumers to appeal insurance company decisions. There's also growing pressure for healthcare providers to make their costs and billing practices more transparent to the public.

As things stand now, you can never assume the bills you receive are accurate or fair—it's imperative to review them carefully and question everything. It's not an easy task, but a little information about what can go wrong and how to deal with it can go a long way toward saving you and your family a lot of money.

CHAPTER 8

Medicare

Understanding Your Benefits and Choosing the Right Plan

There's a lot to know when it comes to signing up for Medicare. This chapter will help you understand how Medicare works, and how to choose the right plan for yourself or a loved one.

Medicare Basics

Medicare covers nearly 50 million Americans aged 65 and older, as well as people younger than 65 who have disabilities.[1]

It's a health insurance program run by the federal government. Yet, in many ways coverage is similar to that of private health insurance.

Before discussing the details of when to sign up, how to choose the right plan for you, and using your benefits, let's start by going over a few basics about Medicare.

Medicare and Its Parts

Why is Medicare so confusing to so many people? It could be because it has a number of different parts, each covering different types of medical services with different annual deductibles, co-payments, and monthly premiums.

---

[1] Kaiser Family Foundation: Medicare, www.kff.org/medicare/

There are four parts of Medicare you need to know about:[2]

1. Medicare Part A

Medicare Part A helps you pay for hospital stays. Nursing facility care that's needed for a short period following a stay in the hospital and limited home health and hospice care services are also covered by Medicare Part A.

If you or your spouse worked for at least 10 years and paid Social Security taxes, Part A will be free to you. Even if you haven't paid taxes for 10 years, you can still get Medicare Part A. However, you'll pay a monthly premium for it. In 2013, the premium is $248 each month if you (or your spouse) worked and paid Medicare taxes in the U.S. for a period of 7.5 to 10 years. That cost increases to $441 each month if you spent fewer than 7.5 years working and paying Medicare taxes.

COST ALERT!

With Medicare Part A, you'll be responsible for a co-payment each time you are admitted to the hospital. Each benefit period comes with a $1,184 deductible. And, after 60 days in the hospital, there's a daily charge of $296, which shoots up to $592 daily if you're hospitalized for more than 90 days.

A little further on in this chapter we'll talk about options to purchase supplementary coverage to help take care of these additional costs and how you can protect yourself from steep medical bills.

---

2. Medicare Part B

Most medically necessary doctor visits, laboratory and imaging tests, such as X-rays and MRIs, as well as outpatient mental health services are covered by Medicare Part B. So are medical equipment and supplies, some home health care, and ambulance rides. Unlike Part A, there is a monthly premium attached to Medicare Part B. In 2013 the standard rate is $104.90 per month.

If you have a higher income you'll pay more for Part B (Table 8-1).

---

[2]Medicare.gov

Table 8-1. Medicare Part B Monthly Premiums

If your yearly income in 2011 was		You pay (in 2013)
Filing individual tax return	Filing joint tax return	
$85,000 or less	$170,000 or less	$104.90
above $85,000 up to $107,000	above $170,000 up to $214,000	$146.90
above $107,000 up to $160,000	above $214,000 up to $320,000	$209.80
above $160,000 up to $214,000	above $320,000 up to $428,000	$272.70
above $214,000	above $428,000	$335.70

Source: Medicare.gov

Jargon Alert Both Medicare Parts A and B comprise what is often referred to as "Original Medicare." This is the traditional fee-for-service program provided by the federal government. With Original Medicare, you do not need permission from an insurance company before seeking care. You can go directly to any doctor or hospital that accepts Medicare payment.

3. Medicare Part C

Medicare Part C, also called Medicare Advantage, allows private insurance companies approved by the government to provide Medicare benefits.

Medicare Advantage plans are required to offer the same services as both Medicare Parts A and B. Often, they also include drug coverage (Medicare Part D) along with extras that don't come with Original Medicare (which, again, includes Medicare Parts A and B) such as vision and dental coverage. You can think of these plans as a bundle of all the pieces of Medicare.

If you have a private health plan now through work or one you buy on your own, such as a Health Maintenance Organization (HMO) or Preferred Provider Organization (PPO), a Medicare Advantage plan will seem very familiar to you.

Unlike Original Medicare, which allows you to see any doctor participating in the Medicare program, with Part C, you typically need to use healthcare providers and pharmacies within the plan's network. There are many Medicare Advantage plans to choose from. Some come with an extra monthly cost while others require no additional payment at all (you'll still pay your Part B premium, however).

With a Medicare Advantage plan, there are caps placed on your total out-of-pocket costs; you won't spend more than **$6,700** in 2013, not including your prescription drug costs.

■ **Note** As with Medicare Part A, there are additional costs when you visit the doctor or use other outpatient medical services. There's an annual deductible of $147 and a 20% co-pay each time you receive care.[3]

NEW BENEFITS UNDER HEALTH REFORM

The Affordable Care Act provides free annual wellness visits and screening tests, such as mammograms and diabetes screenings. Co-pays, co-insurance and deductibles are all waived at the time of the visit.

4. Medicare Part D

To get help paying for prescription drug costs you need to sign up for a Medicare Part D plan. Part D is optional; you aren't required to have it. But unless you have another type of insurance—say through your job or your spouse's job—to help pay for the cost of medications, you should sign on for a plan when you're eligible.

Part D prescription drug plans are offered by private insurance companies that are paid by the government to provide services. There are monthly premiums attached to Part D plans as well, which vary depending on the plan you choose.

NEW BENEFITS UNDER HEALTH REFORM

If you take a lot of medications, you're likely familiar with the donut hole—the gap in prescription drug coverage that leaves seniors on the hook for their total drug costs within that gap. Because of the Affordable Care Act, name-brand drug costs are slashed by 52.5% and 21% for generics once you hit the donut hole. Discounts will grow to 75% by the year 2020.[4]

---

[3]Medicare Interactive.org: http://www.medicareinteractive.org/page2.php?topic=counselor&page=script&slide_id=552
[4]Medicare Rights Center: Closing the Donut Hole: www.medicarerights.org/pdf/Closing-the-Doughnut-Hole-Chart.pdf

Medigap

Medicare alone does not pay for all health care services. That's why many people opt for a supplemental Medicare insurance plan called Medigap or sign on to the Medicare Advantage plans as discussed earlier.

Medigap supplements Original Medicare—you must be signed up for both Medicare Parts A and B—and helps to cover the cost of co-payments, deductibles, and other out-of-pocket expenses.

Medigap policies are offered by private insurance companies, and they come with an additional monthly cost. There are 10 plans available for purchase (Plans A, B, C, D, F, G, K, L, M, and N; plus Massachusetts, Minnesota, and Wisconsin have their own Medigap policies). Because the plans must comply with federal and state laws, they are all very similar. The main difference among them, in fact, tends to be price, which is why shopping around is important.[5]

Also important to understand is that the rates for Medigap plans are determined in one of two ways:

1. **Community rating:** Rates are influenced by where you live.
2. **Age rating:** Rates are influenced by your age.

Although more expensive at the start, your long-term costs are likely to be lower when you buy a community-rated, rather than age-rated product.

COST ALERT!

Medicare Parts A and B alone will not pay for all of your costs. Without additional coverage, either through a Medigap or Medicare Advantage plan, there is no limit to how much you may be required to spend on your medical care.

When to Sign Up

Most people become eligible for Medicare when they turn 65. There's a seven-month window for signing up for Medicare that opens three months before your 65th birthday, then extends through your birth month, and for three months after (Figure 8-1).

---

[5] Medicare.gov

Chapter 8 | Medicare

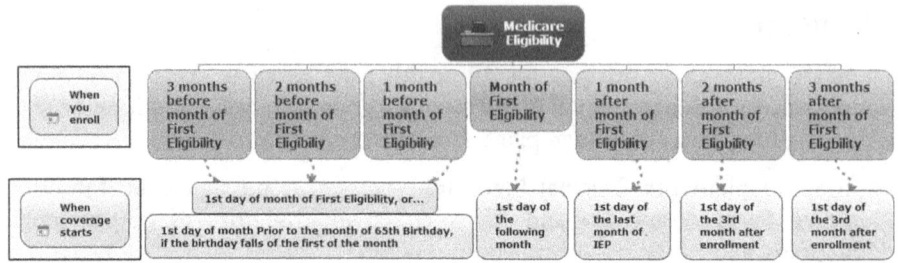

Figure 8-1. Medicare Eligibility
Source: eHealth

If by the time you turn 65 you're already collecting Social Security, you will automatically be signed up for Medicare Part A (inpatient coverage). You should expect your Medicare card three months before your birthday (Figure 8-2).

Figure 8-2. A typical Medicare insurance card
Source: Medicare.gov

■ **Resource Alert** To enroll in Medicare, call the Social Security Administration at 800-772-1213. You can also connect online at www.ssa.gov or visit your local Social Security office.

Avoid Penalties

The government wants to make sure that all Americans sign up for Medicare coverage as soon as they are eligible, as opposed to waiting until they become sick. That's why a penalty fee is added to Medicare Part A, Medicare Part B, and Medicare Part D if you fail to enroll on time. In some cases, the penalties can be life-long, meaning once you've incurred the fee, it will be added to the cost of your Medicare benefits for the rest of your life. For that reason, you need to be aware of the penalties and how to avoid them.

Paying Up for Part B

Unlike Part A, to receive Medicare Part B benefits you have to actively sign yourself up. If you fail to do so when you're first eligible, you'll face a financial penalty that sticks with you for life.

Here's how the penalty works:

For every 12 months you're eligible for Part B but don't enroll, you will incur a penalty of 10%. That amount is added onto the current cost of the Part B premium, which is, on average, $104.90 per month in 2013.

That means if you wait until you're 67 to sign up for Medicare Part B—two years after you're first eligible—you'll pay 20% more than you would have if you signed up on time (10% × the 2 years you delayed).

Still working at 65? If your job offers you health insurance or you're covered by your spouse's work-based coverage, you don't necessarily need to sign on to Part B. In many cases, though certainly not all, the work-based insurance you have offers the coverage you need. However, that's not the case if you work for a company with fewer than 20 employees. If you're employed by a small firm, you'll need to sign onto Medicare once you turn 65 to avoid penalties.

Resource Alert Medicare.gov has a Medicare Part B Late Enrollment Calculator to help you figure out exactly how much of a penalty you'll pay for late Part B enrollment. Once you lose your work-based coverage, you have an eight-month window to enroll before the penalty kicks into place.

Part D Penalties

If you have drug coverage through your employer, there's no need to buy into Medicare Part D as long as the coverage is considered to be "creditable," meaning it's comparable to what Medicare pays for. However, once that coverage goes away, you have just 63 days to buy a Part D plan. Further delay will cost you 1% above the average national cost of a prescription drug plan for every month you were eligible and didn't sign up.

Jargon Alert *Creditable Coverage* refers to prescription drug coverage that pays on average as much as the standard Medicare prescription drug plan.

Medigap

If you're interested in a Medigap plan, you need to sign up within the first six months of becoming eligible for Medicare. After that, insurers can take the state of your health into consideration when deciding whether or not to sell you a plan. That means you can be denied coverage, leaving you on the hook for potentially high costs when you need medical care.

HEALTH REFORM AND BUYING COVERAGE ON YOUR OWN

If you buy your own health insurance, rather than get it through your job, starting in 2014, you will be able to buy your coverage through one of the online state-based insurance markets that will be live in October 2013 as part of the new health reform law.

If you buy your insurance this way, once you become eligible for Medicare you'll need to sign up for it right away.

Annual Enrollment Periods

Once you're covered by Medicare, there are a few annual events you should know about.

General Enrollment: If you don't sign up for either Medicare Part A or Part B when you're first eligible to do so, you'll have a chance to sign up between January 1 and March 31 every year.

Open Enrollment: Between October 15 and December 7 anyone with a Medicare Advantage plan (Part C) or a Part D prescription drug plan can change his or her coverage by selecting a new plan that will take effect on January 1 of the following calendar year.

During this time you can:

- Enroll in a Part D prescription drug plan
- Switch from one Part D plan to another
- Drop a Medicare Advantage plan and return to Original Medicare
- Enroll in a Medicare Advantage plan for the first time
- Change from one Medicare Advantage plan to another

Disenrollment: Unhappy with your Medicare Advantage Plan? If so, between January 1 and February 14 each year you have the option of dropping your existing coverage and returning to Original Medicare. You'll also be allowed to sign on to a Part D prescription drug plan.

If you go back to Original Medicare, however, you'll also need to pick up supplemental insurance—a Medigap plan—to help cover the cost of co-payments, deductibles, and other out-of-pocket expenses that can get very pricey. But consider this decision very carefully. Remember, Medigap plans can deny your enrollment outside of your first six months of eligibility for Medicare.

There are other details to watch for when switching during the disenrollment period from Medicare Advantage back to Original Medicare to make sure your medical needs will be met at a price you can afford.

Be sure that:

1. The plan includes benefits that will meet your medical needs.
2. Your doctor and hospitals near you accept Original Medicare.
3. Your prescription medications are covered by the Part D plan in which you want to enroll.
4. There are pharmacies close to you participating with your health plan's network.

5-Star Special Enrollment Period: Because of the Affordable Care Act, Medicare began to rate the quality of both Medicare Advantage and Part D plans. Medicare plans can earn anywhere from one to five stars, with five stars representing the highest rating (see the resource list later in this chapter for websites where you can compare plans and view their start ratings).

From December 8 through November 30 you'll be given extra time to sign up for Medicare Advantage and Part D prescription drug plans that earn the top five-star rating. During this period, you can also switch from a lower-rated plan to one that has earned five stars.

You can see the various plans available to you in your area and their star ratings at:

- Medicare.gov
- eHealthMedicare.com
- Healthpocket.com

Medicare Advantage or Medigap?

We talked earlier in this chapter about the fact that Original Medicare won't cover all your costs. To gain more coverage, either a Medigap or Medicare Advantage plan is needed. Selecting the right option for yourself can make a big difference in how much you ultimately spend on your medical care. So, how do you know which plan to go with?

Take a look at Figure 8-3 to see your options when deciding how you'd like to get Medicare coverage.

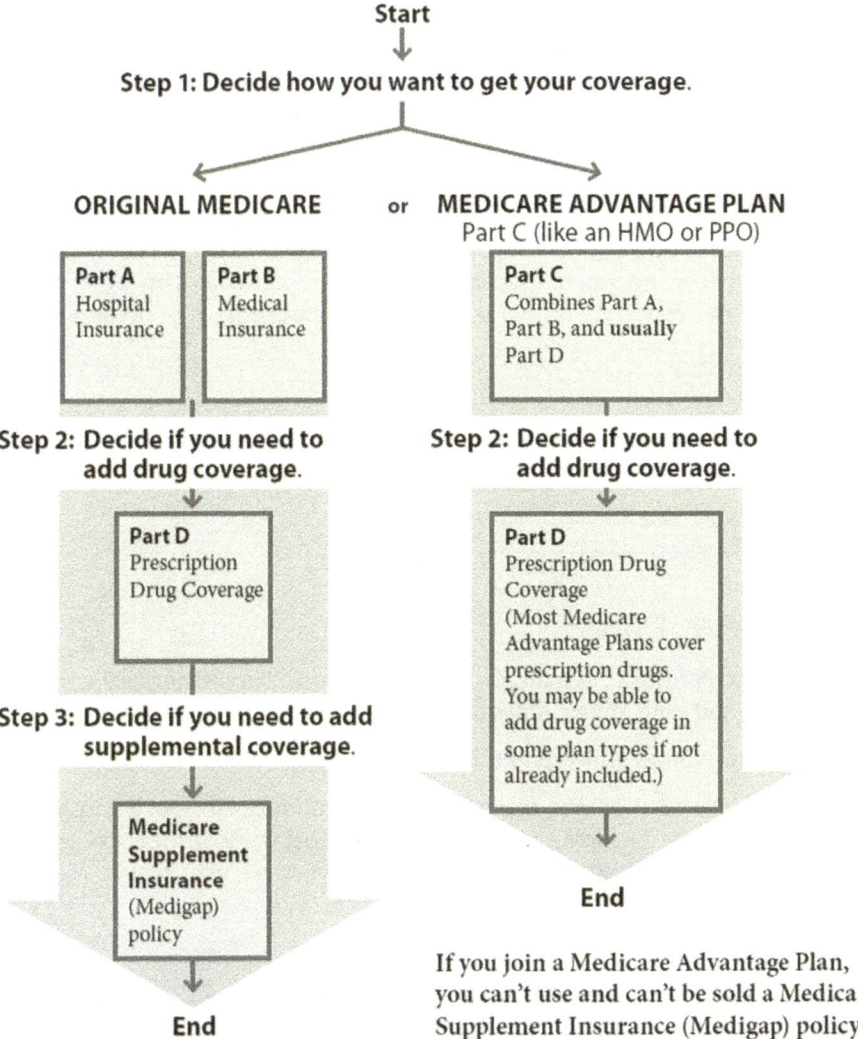

Figure 8-3. Options for Medicare coverage
Source: *Medicare.gov*

Here are a few questions to ask yourself:

What Type of Benefits Are Most Important to Me?

Often, Medicare Advantage plans provide more than just Part A (hospital coverage) Part B (outpatient care) and Part D (prescription drug coverage). Some also provide dental coverage, vision care, and wellness programs that give you free gym memberships and other benefits. Does this matter to you? Do you need or want these additional benefits?

Do You Move Around?

If retirement means splitting your time between cities, Medicare Advantage is likely not for you. Instead, consider going with Original Medicare with a Part D prescription drug plan and a Medigap policy to cover additional costs such as co-pays, deductibles, and other out-of-pocket costs.

Here's the reason why: With Original Medicare, coverage doesn't depend on you seeing a healthcare provider who participates in a particular insurance company provider network. Medicare Advantage plans, on the other hand, may not pay for your care if you seek treatment outside of your designated network.

Jargon Alert *Provider Network* refers to the doctors, hospitals, laboratories and other healthcare providers who have signed contracts agreeing to work with your insurance company. These healthcare providers are often referred to as "in-network."

What Does It Cost?

In order to select the best plan for you, you need to simultaneously consider your budget and your medical needs.

Here are some things to keep in mind:

In 2013, Medicare Advantage plans have a maximum out-of-pocket spending limit of $6,700 (not including prescription drug costs). Most Medigap policies cover more of your costs. However, they tend to come with higher monthly premiums than Medicare Advantage plans.

Resource Alert Medicare Savings Programs (MSPs) help low-income seniors cover the cost of Medicare Part B premiums for outpatient care and may also help with co-pays, co-insurance and deductibles. Medicare Extra Help offers assistance paying for Part D premiums. To see if you qualify, check benefitscheckup.org or call Medicare: 800-MEDICARE.

Do You Take Medications?

Medicare Advantage plans typically include prescription drug coverage. That means all of your medical care is handled by one umbrella plan. If you have Original Medicare, you'll also need to buy a Part D plan if you want help paying for your prescription medications.

> **Tip** Spend 6 months in New York and 6 months in Florida? Medicare Advantage probably isn't a good bet for you. Such plans generally tie you to a physician network in a particular locale.

Signing Up for Medicare When You're Still Working

It's commonly thought that 65 is this country's average retirement age. But today, the average American expects to retire at age 67—seven years later than in the mid-1990s, according to the opinion research company Gallup.[6]

If you plan to stay on the job past the age of 65 and will continue to have health insurance from a company with 20 or more employees, you may not need to sign up for Medicare right away. (If your company employs fewer than 20 people, you must sign up for Medicare when you're first eligible.)

There are a number of factors to consider when thinking about when and whether and which parts of Medicare to sign up for if you still have work-based insurance coverage. Here's a rundown.

Sign on for Part A. Because there's no cost to sign up for Part A, you should enroll when you're first eligible. If you are hospitalized, there's a chance that Medicare will cover the cost of services not paid for by your employer-based insurance.

Do the math on Parts B and D. Since Medicare Parts B and D both come with a monthly premium, it may not pay to sign up when you first turn 65, since your employer-sponsored insurance is likely to duplicate the coverage.

To determine whether or not buying in at this point makes sense, calculate your current spending on outpatient healthcare. Are you spending more than the cost of the Part B premium?

If you're spending more each month on co-pays and deductibles for outpatient care than the $104.90 it costs for the Part B premium, it makes sense to sign up now to get help paying for medical expenses your employer's health plan does not. If your costs are less than the Part B premium, however, you can wait. Because you have employer-sponsored health insurance, you won't be hit with the Part B penalty that comes with signing up late when you have no other health insurance coverage.

---

[6]Gallup: www.gallup.com/poll/154178/expected-retirement-age.aspx

Should you buy a Part D drug coverage plan? Compare the coverage you get on the job against that provided by Medicare Part D plans. If your employer offers coverage that is comparable to the plan you'd purchase, it's likely not necessary for you to buy into Medicare prescription drug coverage.

Just make sure you confirm each year with your employer that the plan you're being offered at work is considered "creditable." (Again, meaning it provides coverage comparable to Medicare.) If it's not, you're going to get hit with a penalty for signing up late.

Remember time limits. Once you decide to retire and no longer get insurance through your employer, you'll have eight months to sign up for Medicare Part B and just 63 days to sign onto Part D before incurring a late penalty.

Forget your spouse. If you've been covered by employer-sponsored health insurance for years and you're married, there's a good chance you've grown accustomed to including your spouse and/or your kids on your health plan as dependents.

Medicare operates differently.

When spouses are of different ages and the person supplying the work-based insurance coverage is the older of the two, the couple will need to part ways insurance-wise when one of them signs onto Medicare. There is no dependent coverage under the Medicare program.

For more information about signing up for Medicare while you're still working, look for The Medicare Rights Center guide: *How Medicare Works with Employer-Based Insurance: A Guide for Employers, Professionals and Consumers* (Medicarerights.org).

Getting Help

Medicare is a complicated program and one with which you're likely to need some personal assistance. Here's where you can go for help:

- State Health Insurance Counseling and Assistance Programs (SHIPS) provide Medicare recipients free access to counselors who will help you compare Medicare plans and choose the best option for you. To find the SHIPS office near you, visit Medicare.gov or call 800-MEDICARE (800-633-4227). On this Web page, you'll also find links to other helpful resources.

- Medicare.gov offers information and resources for finding Medicare drug and health plans, as well as Medigap policies on its Medicare Plan Finder tool.
- Mymedicalmatters.org, a website run by the National Council on Aging, provides information about Medicare drug plans as well as how to evaluate your needs and sign up for coverage. The Council also offers a benefits checkup tool where you can find and enroll in federal, state, local, and private programs that help pay for prescription drugs, utility bills, meals, healthcare, and other needs.
- The Center for Medicare Advocacy is a nonprofit, nonpartisan education and advocacy organization that has a wealth of information on its website about the various parts of Medicare as well as associated costs.

Additional websites for shopping for Medicare plans include:
- Planprescriber.com, and
- Healthpocket.com

Finding Help in Paying for Medicare Costs

If you're having difficulty paying for your Medicare-related costs, there is help available. Medicare Savings Programs (MSPs) provide people with low income and limited assets help covering expenses associated with Medicare Part A and Part B, including premiums, co-pays, co-insurance, and deductibles.[7] You can find the MSP program in your state by logging onto the Medicare.gov Medicare Savings Program page at: www.medicare.gov/Contacts/static-pages/msps.aspx.

Avoiding Costly Pitfalls

There are a number of ways in which people end up paying extra costs or lose out on important Medicare benefits, often unnecessarily. Here are a few common pitfalls to watch for:

---

[7] Medicare.gov, Medicare Savings Program: www.medicare.gov/your-medicare-costs/help-paying-costs/medicare-savings-program/medicare-savings-programs.html#slmb

You Don't Shop Your Options

As I discuss earlier in this chapter, if you have a Medicare Advantage or Part D prescription drug plan, you'll have an opportunity to re-evaluate and change your existing coverage during the open enrollment period that runs each year between October 15 and December 7.

The fact is that too few people take the time to examine their existing coverage to make sure important changes haven't been made to their plan or to consider that other options that would better serve their needs and/or save them money are available.

According to a survey by PlanPrescriber, an online provider of free Medicare education and plan comparison tools, the average Medicare beneficiary spent an additional $600 or more in 2012 because he or she was in the wrong plan. Only 13% percent of customers were in the Medicare Advantage plan with the lowest total out-of-pocket costs; only 5% were in the Part D with the lowest total out-of-pocket costs.

When shopping for the best price and mix of benefits you need to take into account all of your costs, including:

- Your monthly premium
- Co-pays
- Co-insurance
- Deductibles
- Maximum out-of-pocket costs

Observation Status

How you're classified when you are admitted to the hospital can have a big impact on your finances, as well as on the medical services ultimately available to you.

In past years, there's been a growing concern that people with Medicare are more routinely hospitalized for days, yet not considered an "inpatient" or having been officially admitted to the hospital. Instead, their stay is classified to indicate they are receiving "observation services." With observation services the idea is to *observe* the patient so doctors can determine whether someone needs to be admitted to the hospital.

Observation services are considered outpatient care, not inpatient. Why does all this matter? Several reasons:

It will cost you. Because observation services are considered outpatient care, it will be billed under Medicare Part B, the part of Medicare that pays for outpatient services. Hospital charges for an observation stay are often billed separately and can include the cost of room and board in blocks of time. What's more, Medicare will not pay for the care you're provided by doctors while under observation.

Here's how that plays out for your finances.

Consider that in 2012 the average cost for a hospital stay was $14,662.

- *Under Part A:* Your bill for a $14,662 hospital admission could be as little as $1,200 (Part A's deductible is about $1,200).
- *Under Part B:* Your bill for a $14,662 hospital admission could be as much as $2,900 (Part B's deductible is about $160 and co-insurance is 20%).[8]

It limits your coverage. Medicare will pay for 20 days of skilled nursing facility (SNF) care, but only following three consecutive days in the hospital.

That means if you've been "under observation" for even some part of your stay, you won't qualify for nursing home care coverage. The full cost of SNF care will be your responsibility.

Often, you have to ask about your status to know. Don't be surprised if the hospital doesn't notify you.

Here are some simple steps you can take:[9]

- Ask your doctor whether you've been officially admitted as an inpatient or are in observation status.
- If you are in observation, ask him or her to write an order to admit you to the hospital as an inpatient.
- Confirm the change has been made. Having your status altered after you've left the hospital can be very difficult.
- Get help. You can visit www.medicare.gov/publications to view the booklet "Your Medicare Rights and Protections." Or call 1-800-MEDICARE (1-800-633-4227).

---

[8] PlanPrescriber
[9] Medicare.gov: www.medicare.gov/Pubs/pdf/11435.pdf

Summary

Medicare coverage is an important benefit for American seniors as well as millions of people living with disabilities.

As with any form of insurance, understanding how to best use your benefits, what is and is not covered, and where to turn for help when your options are hard to understand can make all the difference in your ability to access and pay for needed care.

Although Medicare pays for many important services, it won't cover all your needs. In the next chapter I'll talk about making plans for the future, including planning for the possibility of long-term care needs as you age.

CHAPTER 9

Taking Charge of Your Healthcare Future
Planning Ahead

As much as we may like to avoid considering the possibility that we or a loved one will someday become disabled, disability and end-of-life care are things we'd be well served to think about before a crisis hits.

Getting Your Affairs in Order

Most of us dream our golden years will be just that. We picture our older selves in perfect health with sharp minds well into our 80s and beyond, with undiminished energy and the time, at last, to pursue long-deferred interests.

Sadly, the dream becomes reality for only a very fortunate few. You might be among them if you are blessed with great genes or have followed your doctor's advice to eat well, exercise, avoid tobacco, and in general practice moderation.

Then again, there are no guarantees.

Chapter 9 | Taking Charge of Your Healthcare Future

For most people, aging brings health declines and hard decisions. Knowing what to expect and planning ahead can make the difficult road much easier for you and your loved ones.

Healthcare Advance Directives: Getting Your Affairs in Order

An advance directive is a document that outlines a person's wishes for healthcare decisions in the event that he or she at some point in the future becomes unable to make decisions for him- or herself.[1]

Though many people prefer not to think about the possibility of becoming so debilitated that they can no longer manage their own affairs, it's more common than most of us want to acknowledge.

Tom and John Sharp had plenty of time to talk to their dad Joe about his financial affairs during his year-and-a-half-long battle with throat cancer, but it was a conversation no one really wanted to have.

During two lengthy rounds of chemotherapy and months of hospice care, their many conversations centered on other serious and not-so-serious topics, including their shared love of golf, college basketball, and Major League Baseball.

When he died at 74, Joe Sharp fortunately had legal documents in place to guide the settlement of his complicated financial interests, which included a business and multiple properties. And both he and his wife had living wills that spelled out their healthcare wishes.

"The big things were taken care of," his oldest son Tom says. "It was the little things that we had to figure out later. We spent a lot of time trying to find the car titles, for example."

Caring for sick loved ones often involves dealing with both physical needs and financial responsibilities.

Having key documents in place and knowing where to find them helps. Without these documents, family members may have no rights under the law to manage investments, deposit checks, pay taxes, or handle other legal matters.

---

[1]Patients Right Council. Advance Directives: Definitions: www.patientsrightscouncil.org/site/advance-directives-definitions/

If someone becomes mentally impaired without having legal structures in place for handling his or her affairs, the person is left vulnerable to fraud and theft.

Though planning for your inevitable end may not sound like much fun, putting your affairs in order with legal documents known as advance directives is one of the best things you can do for yourself and your loved ones.

Having these legal documents increases the chances that you will receive the medical care you desire if you can no longer make your wishes known, and that your loved ones are protected financially.

There are two types of advance directives—those that deal with financial matters and those that deal with health issues.

Financial Advance Directives

Let's look at the two main types of financial advance directives.

The Durable Power of Attorney for Financial Matters

This document allows you to appoint someone to make financial decisions for you when you are not able to make them for yourself. The power can be very broad, giving another the authority to make all financial decisions on your behalf. Or it can be limited, giving another the right only to sell your car or some other property, for example.

Trusts

A trust clearly sets the rules for the assets held in trust that you want followed either during your lifetime if you become incapacitated or disabled or after your death. The rules are enforced by a trustee chosen by you.

In addition to selecting the person you want to manage your affairs, it's important to think about other people in your life who could gain access to information about your finances and whether you want to put controls in place that grant or deny permission to know the details of your financial life.

If, for example, you choose one of your three children as your trustee, would you want him or her to share information with your two other children? Do you want your accountant or attorney to receive financial reports? The trust should be specific to this level of detail as to who can and cannot be involved so only those you want to be informed of your affairs will get the information.

Advance Care Directives

There are two main healthcare advance directives

Living Wills

Living wills spell out the type of medical care you want if you are incapacitated, such as if you are in a coma. Would you want to remain on life support if you had severe brain damage? Under what circumstances would you not want to be kept alive? When would you want to have breathing assistance, a feeding tube, or even certain medications, and when would you not want these life-support measures? Living wills can address any of these issues, depending on your wishes.

Durable Power of Attorney for Healthcare

This document names someone who will make any and all healthcare decisions for you when you are no longer able to make them for yourself. It also gives the named caregiver access to your medical records.

It is a good idea to have both of these documents, says attorney Gregory S. French, who is president of the National Academy of Elder Law Attorneys.

"Living wills really only deal with life and death issues," he says. "A lot of people think they cover many more situations than they do. That's why it is important to name someone to make healthcare decisions for you if you can't make them for yourself."

Some states allow the two documents to be merged into one, but others don't. Most states do allow specific wishes to be included in a healthcare power of attorney, however.

"There can be a lot of customizing of these documents," French says.

Because of this and because laws vary from state to state, it's a good idea to consult a lawyer who specializes in trusts and estates to set up advance directives.

It's also a good idea to review advance directives every five years at a minimum as well as any time there is a significant change in your health status.[2]

---

[2]National Academy of Elder Law Attorneys. Health Care Decision Making: Public Policy Guidelines: http://bit.ly/11UCV2m

There are a number of online resources where you can learn more about advance directives and get help setting them up:

- To find an attorney who can help you set up the documents you need, contact:
  - National Academy of Elder Law Attorneys' online directory, which is a good resource for finding attorneys specializing in elder care (www.naela.org), or
  - The American Bar Association (www.americanbar.org)
- To easily set up advance directives and living wills online visit the Five Wishes program available on the website of the nonprofit organization Aging with Dignity (www.agingwithdignity.org/five-wishes.php)
- Help4srs.org provides information about healthcare documents, estate planning, and more.
- You can download advance directives for each state at the National Hospice and Palliative Care Organization's Caring Connections website (www.caringinfo.org)—they can be filled out without the help of an attorney.

The Cost of Alzheimer's: What's Covered, What's Not

Five-and-a-half million Americans are age 85 or older, and this number is projected to triple during the next four decades.[3]

Not surprisingly, the number of Americans with Alzheimer's disease and other age-related dementias is expected to almost triple as well.

In a recent study supported by the Alzheimer's Association and the National Institute on Aging, researchers concluded that close to 14 million people in the United States will have Alzheimer's-related dementia in 2050, compared to around 5 million today.[4]

Nine out of ten Alzheimer's patients are older than the age of 65, but unlike its coverage for a number of other illnesses affecting the elderly, Medicare doesn't pay for many of the expenses families incur when caring for a loved one with the disease.

And the expenses can be overwhelming: According to the Alzheimer's Association, the cost of caring for a person with Alzheimer's disease is

---

[3] AgingStats.gov. www.agingstats.gov/Main_Site/Data/2012_Documents/Population.aspx
[4] Herbert, LE. *Neurology*, February 6, 2013.

nearly $57,000 a year. Most of that cost—60%, in fact—falls on a family's shoulders.[5]

Knowing what Medicare covers and what it doesn't, before services are needed, is critical for long-term financial planning.

Doctor's Visits Are Covered, Along with Other Outpatient Medical Services

These services include visits to internists, specialists, and physical and speech therapists. Lab tests are also paid for by Medicare Part B.

Under the Affordable Care Act, an annual wellness visit, which includes a medical evaluation to determine if there has been a decline in memory or other cognitive functioning, is also covered.

With traditional Medicare, patients pay 20% of the cost of outpatient medical visits, but supplemental insurance programs such as Medigap plans can help cover these out-of-pocket costs.[6]

Long-Term Nursing Home Care: Not Covered by Medicare

The biggest drain on the budgets of most families is paying for nursing home care when it is needed. Long-term nursing home care can cost $60,000 to $200,000 a year, depending on where you live.[7]

Medicare does pay for some short-term nursing care, but only up to 100 days following a hospital stay of three days or more. However, Medicare does not pay for long-term nursing home care, which people with advanced dementia often require.

We'll cover methods for paying for long-term care later on in this chapter.

In-Home Services: Might Be Covered

Regular in-home services may be covered by Medicare if they are deemed medically necessary and involve a nurse, therapist, or other skilled healthcare worker.

This type of care does not have to occur every day, but it does need to be scheduled on a regular basis. Even once a week can be enough to get coverage.

---

[5] Alzheimer's Association. The Shriver Report: www.alz.org/shriverreport/about.html
[6] Medicare.gov. www.medicare.gov/Pubs/pdf/02110.pdf
[7] AARP. http://assets.aarp.org/external_sites/caregiving/options/nursing_home_costs.html

Unfortunately, many Alzheimer's patients also need unskilled adult day care that is not covered by Medicare. In-home care that involves having someone come into the home to help a loved one with bathing, eating, getting dressed, and other daily activities can be very pricey—$100 a day or more.

Most Drugs: Probably Covered

Most medications for people with Alzheimer's disease are covered under Medicare Part D prescription drug plans, but it is important to know your co-payment and your insurance plan's rules regarding pre approval. Also, make sure your pharmacy is in the plan's network before having prescriptions filled.

Part D drug plan costs can be compared using the Medicare Plan Finder tool (www.medicare.gov/find-a-plan).

The Alzheimer's Association also offers a coverage guide for common Alzheimer's drugs (www.alz.org).

Other online resources for Alzheimer's help include:

- The National Institute on Aging Alzheimer's Disease Education and Referral Center (www.nia.nih.gov/alzheimers)
- Medicare Rights Center (www.medicarerights.org/)
- The Center for Medicare Advocacy (www.medicareadvocacy.org/)
- The Administration on Aging (www.aoa.gov)
- The Alzheimer's Resource Center (www.alzheimersresourcecenter.org)

Long-Term Care Insurance

Long-term care insurance once seemed like a perfect vehicle to give aging Baby Boomers peace of mind, but as premiums continue to climb it is becoming more important to carefully evaluate whether long-term care insurance makes sense as you consider ways to help pay for the cost of home health or nursing care in the years ahead.

Consider This!

Long-term care insurance policies typically cover things that Medicare doesn't pay for, such as expenses associated with extended home care, assisted living, and nursing homes.

Most policies have a waiting period, so when a policyholder needs a home health nurse or enters a nursing home, the cost of services won't be covered for the first 90 to 120 days.

According to 2013 figures from the American Association for Long-Term Care Insurance, a 55-year-old buying long-term care insurance can expect to pay around $2,065 a year for $162,000 of benefits. With inflation, those benefits will grow to $330,000 of coverage by the time the policyholder reaches age 80.[8]

On average, a 60-year-old couple can expect to pay around $3,700 a year for an inflation-adjusted policy that will pay $329,000 each in benefits when they turn 85 (at an estimated inflation rate of 3% compounded annually).

Some insurers offer less expensive premiums for policies that do not adjust for inflation, but the payouts are not likely to cover the full cost of care when it is needed.

But the big question is: Do you need long-term care insurance?

The reality is that most of us do. Statistics show that 70% of people who reach the age of 65 will need long-term care before they die.

And nursing home care is often extremely pricey: According to a 2012 Kiplinger's report on retirement, the cost of nursing-home care averaged more than $87,000 a year in 2011.[9]

When it comes to paying for nursing home care, Medicaid—the joint state and federal health program that pays for certain health services and nursing home care for people with limited income and resources—covers the cost of care for roughly 7 out of every 10 nursing home residents.

To qualify for Medicaid, you may have to spend a lot of your own money on medical care and significantly reduce your assets.[10] To protect yourself and your loved ones financially, it's best to consider options in advance to pay for nursing services.

The Cost of Care Is High

Long-term care can cost as much as $250 a day, so it doesn't take long to deplete a lifetime of savings.[11]

---

[8]American Association for Long-Term Care Insurance Price Index. www.aaltci.org/
[9]*Kiplinger's Retirement Report*, Volume 19, Number 5, May, 2012.
www.neamb.com/assets/documents/1205.pdf
[10]Medicare.gov
[11]Wall Street Journal. Should You Purchase Long-Term Care Insurance?
http://online.wsj.com/article/SB10001424052702303425504577352031401783756.html

Here are some details to consider with regard to purchasing a long-term care insurance policy at a price you can afford.

Consider your age. When it comes to buying long-term care insurance, the younger you are when you buy, the more affordable it is. Generally, experts recommend buying a policy no later than in your 50s.

Look to your employer. Like most health-related benefits, getting long-term care insurance through your job is often less expensive than buying it on your own. If you don't already know, check with your employer to see if buying into a long-term care policy is available at work. In some cases, the premiums you pay can be deducted from your taxes, thereby lowering your costs.

Prepare for rising costs. Those who already own long-term care insurance are probably facing rising premiums. Most major companies such as John Hancock, Prudential, and MetLife have imposed significant hikes in the cost of coverage over the past few years on existing policyholders, leaving many people wondering if it makes sense to keep the insurance.

As a natural response, many people consider dropping the plans they currently have. But doing so means all the money you've paid into the policy for years has gone to waste. You'll have spent thousands of dollars and be left with no benefits to show for it.

However, if you're committed to having a long-term care policy, you should realize that though the rate increases are steep, in most cases, paying the inflated premium still costs less than what it would to buy a new long-term care insurance policy in today's marketplace.

Lower your existing costs. If you have long-term care insurance, instead of dropping it, look for ways to lower your premium. There are a number of ways to do that:

- **Reduce your plan's benefit period.** Consider that the average length of stay in a nursing home is about three years. Therefore, if you're paying for a lifetime benefit you may be wasting money. Consider reducing the benefit to three to five years, which will reduce your premium while giving you the level of benefits you're likely to need.

- **Reduce the policy's daily benefit payout, benefit period, or inflation rate.**[12] Keep in mind that over the years the inflation rate of the policy—the amount the benefit increases over time so that benefits keep up with the cost of services—has been 5% per year.

---

[12]Journal of Financial Planning. 2013 5 Ways to Handle a Long-Term Care Insurance Rate Increase.

- **Shared benefit plans.** Married couples have the option of buying a "shared benefit" plan. For example, a three-year shared-benefit policy provides a pool of six years of coverage that can be used as needed between spouses. That means if one spouse needs five years of care and the other needs only one, you're covered. Shared plans are a bit more expensive than two separate plans but you may get more for your money in the long run.[13]

- **Hybrid plans.** Hybrid policies combine long-term-care insurance with either life insurance or annuities. With a life insurance hybrid, for example, you have the option of investing a lump sum of money or paying premiums for ten years. You can use the policy either to cover long-term care costs or to pay a death benefit to your heirs. Any money used toward long- term care would reduce the death benefit.[14]

- **Longevity insurance.** These products require a small investment of money, usually at around age 65, for a large payout at the age of 85. The payout can be used for long-term care or any other expenses you have at that time.[15]

Get professional help. Striking a balance between planning ahead for future healthcare costs and finding a policy you can afford today requires a deft hand. It's always a good idea, for that reason, to work with an experienced insurance professional who specializes in long-term care.

Here are some places where you can find an agent and more information about long-term care insurance:

- American Association of Long-Term Care Insurance (www.aaltci.org/long-term-care-insurance/)
- National Association of Health Underwriters (NAHU.org)
- National Association of Insurance Commissioners (www.naic.org/index_ltc_section.htm) (Look for "A Shopper's Guide to Long-Term Care Insurance")

---

[13]Kiplinger's Retirement Report, Volume 19, Number 5, May 2012.
[14]Ibid.
[15]Ibid.

You can also learn about long-term care options at:
- www.Eldercare.gov
- www.Longtermcare.gov
- www.Caregiver.org

Finding the Right Nursing Home

Choosing a nursing home for a loved one is difficult under the best of circumstances, and circumstances are rarely optimal when decisions about long-term care have to be made.

More often, nursing homes end up being needed after an unexpected health crisis such as a broken hip or a stroke.

Here's what you need to look for to find the best possible nursing home for a loved one.

Learn About Your Options

Before you can make a good selection, you need to get a sense of your nursing home options. There are a few easy ways to find out what's available in your area.

First, ask around. You may have a friend or neighbor who has had a family member who needed long-term care. Moving someone to nursing home care is a big decision, so getting information from people you trust makes sense.

In addition, doctors, nurses, and local hospitals are often good sources of information about the nursing homes in your area. They may also be able to offer recommendations for a good home for your loved one based on his or her condition.

Government websites and agencies are also helpful. Table 10-1 shows some places where you can get help.

Table 10-1. Where to find information on nursing homes.

Organization	How they can help
Area Agencies on Aging (AAAs)	AAAs assist adults age 50 and older and their caregivers. To find the AAA in your area, visit www.eldercare.gov or call The Eldercare Locator at 1-800-677-1116 weekdays from 9:00 a.m. to 8:00 p.m. (EST).
Aging and Disability Resource Centers (ADRCs)	ADRCs assist people of all incomes and ages. Forty-nine states and some territories have ADRCs. To find out if your area is served by an ADRC, visit www.adrc-tae.org.
Centers for Independent Living (CILs)	CILs assist people with disabilities of all incomes and ages. A state-by-state directory of CILs can be found by visiting www.ncil.org/directory.html.
State Technology Assistance Project	The State Technology Assistance Project has information on medical equipment and other assistive technology. Visit www.resna.org or call the Rehabilitation Engineering and Assistive Technology Society of North America (RESNA) at 1-703-524-6686 to get the contact information for your state.
State Medical Assistance (Medicaid) Office	Your State Medical Assistance (Medicaid) office has information about state programs that help pay health and nursing home costs, as well as services in the community, for people with low incomes and limited resources.

Source: Medicare.gov

Evaluate Nursing Home Quality

You can't be too careful when it comes to selecting the right nursing home for a loved one. Knowing where to look when doing your research is critical. Here are a number of resources to tap into.

- **Medicare.gov.** This government website offers a number of resources for learning about nursing homes, including Medicare's comprehensive report: Your Guide to Choosing a Nursing Home (www.medicare.gov/pubs/pdf/02174.pdf). The report includes information on alternatives to nursing home care, as well as resources to help you find certified nursing homes in your area.

- **Nursing Home Compare.** In July of 2012, the Centers for Medicare and Medicaid Services, which certifies the nation's 15,000 nursing homes, made inspection reports for each home available online (www.medicare.gov/nursinghomecompare/). You can compare nursing homes by their ratings of the quality of care each provides (one star is the lowest and five stars the highest rating) in a number of categories. You can also call 1-800-MEDICARE (1-800-633-4227) for that information.

- **Nursing Home Inspect.** This site (http://projects.propublica.org/nursing-homes/), developed by the nonprofit news organization ProPublica, offers data that can be used to compare nursing homes within a state, based on the deficiencies cited by regulators and the penalties imposed over the preceding three years. It can also be used to search more than 60,000 nursing home inspection reports to look for trends and patterns, says co-creator and journalist Charles Ornstein of ProPublica.
- **U.S. News & World Report health website.** *U.S. News* rates more than 15,000 nursing homes throughout the country (http://health.usnews.com/best-nursing-homes) based on key markers of quality including patient safety, health inspection reports, staffing, and more. There is also a state-by-state guide and a step-by-step video on the site with important information on choosing a home. And like the Medicare site, *U.S. News* also has a checklist of questions to ask when you visit nursing homes.

Pay Attention to Staff Turnover

Staff turnover is a key indicator of nursing home quality, but the federal government does not yet require nursing homes to report information about staff retention.

According to the American Health Care Association (AHCA), which represents the nursing home industry, the national average for staff turnover was 39.5% for all nursing home positions in 2010.

In an interview with *U.S. News*, American Health Care Association spokesman Tom Burke said one measure of quality is continuity of care by the nurses and aides who are assigned to residents.

AHCA recommends that individual staffers care for the same residents on at least 80% of their shifts. Burke recommends asking administrators, residents, and their families if this is a priority in the nursing home.

The End of Life: Hospice Care

Hospice is care provided at the end of a person's life, usually when life expectancy is six months or less.

The care focuses on pain management and symptom control, not on aggressive treatment aimed at curing a person's condition.

Hospice is a philosophy of care that emphasizes comfort and support and living life to the fullest in one's final days. It addresses a person's physical pain and symptoms, but also his or her psychological and emotional needs.

Once someone enters hospice care, he or she typically sees a team of healthcare professionals. In addition to the patient's personal physician, the team may include:

- Hospice physicians
- Nurses
- Home health aides
- Social workers
- Clergy

Often, the team makes regular visits to the patient and family to provide additional care, when needed.

Note Hospice care is considered the "gold standard of end-of-life care." Yet, very few people understand the full benefits of these programs.

Options for Receiving Hospice Care

End-of-life care isn't one single thing, and your options for hospice care may depend on where you live.[16]

Hospice care can be delivered at:

- Your home
- Hospitals
- Hospice centers
- Nursing homes
- Other long-term care facilities

---

[16]National Hospice and Palliative Care Organization: www.nhpco.org/

According to the Center to Advance Palliative Care (CAPC) the number of palliative care programs has doubled over the last six years and approximately 1,300 hospitals in the United States have palliative care programs.

Although some hospitals offer their own hospice programs, others still discharge dying patients with no discussion of hospice or palliative care. That means it may be left up to you and your family to find a program in your area.

There are a number of excellent resources available to help you do this, including the doctors, nurses, and social workers treating you or a loved one.

- A state-by-state hospice directory, which can be found at HospiceDirectory.org.
- The National Hospice and Palliative Care Organization (www.nhpco.org)
- The National Hospice Foundation (www.nationalhospicefoundation.org)
- The Hospice Action Network (www.hospiceactionnetwork.org)

Summary

Few of us like to consider the possibility that we or someone we love will one day be too sick to care for or make decisions for ourselves. But the numbers don't lie. Most of us will require some kind of help in the future, and the cost of providing that help is likely to be high.

By taking the time and effort today to plan ahead for the possibility of disability in years to come, we can help to provide greater emotional and financial security for ourselves and the people we love.

APPENDIX A

Consumer Assistance Programs and State Departments of Insurance

State	Contact Information
Alabama	**Alabama Department of Insurance** *Street Address:* 201 Monroe Street, Suite 502 Montgomery, AL 36104 *Mailing Address:* Consumer Services P.O. Box 303351 Montgomery, AL 36130-3351 (334) 241-4141 Insdept@insurance.alabama.gov www.aldoi.gov/ContactUs.aspx

Appendix | Consumer Assistance Programs and State Departments of Insurance

State	Contact Information
Alaska	**Alaska Division of Insurance** *Juneau Office* *Street Address:* 9th Floor, State Office Building 333 Willoughby Avenue Juneau, AK 99801 (907) 465-2515 (800) INSURAK (1-800-467-8725) TDD: (907) 465-5437 *Mailing Address:* P.O. Box 110805 Juneau, AK 99811-0805 *Anchorage Office* *Street Address:* Robert B. Atwood Building 550 W. 7th Avenue, Suite 1560 Anchorage, AK 99501-3567 (907) 269-7900 (800) INSURAK (1-800-467-8725) TDD: (907) 465-5437 www.commerce.state.ak.us/ins/Insurance/consumer.html
American Samoa	**American Samoa Department of Insurance** *Mailing Address:* Office of the Governor American Samoa Government Pago Pago, American Samoa 96799 (684) 633-4116 Fax: (684) 633-2269
Arizona	**Arizona Department of Insurance** *Consumer Services* *Street Address:* 2910 N. 44th Street, Suite 210 Phoenix, AZ 85018-7269 (602) 364-2499 (800) 325-2548 Spanish: (602) 364-2977 www.id.state.az.us consumers@azinsurance.gov

State	Contact Information
Arkansas	**Arkansas Insurance Department** *Consumer Services Division* *Street Address:* 1200 West Third Street Little Rock, AR 72201 (855) 332-2227 Insurance.consumers@arkansas.gov
California	**California Consumer Assistance Program** *Operated by the California Department of Managed Health Care and Department of Insurance* *Street Address:* 980 9th Street, Suite 500 Sacramento, CA 95814 (888) 466-2219 www.HealthHelp.ca.gov
Colorado	**Department of Regulatory Agencies** *Colorado Division of Insurance* *Street Address:* 1560 Broadway, Suite 850 Denver, CO 80202 (800) 930-3745 (303) 894-7490 www.dora.state.co.us/insurance insurance@dora.state.co.us
Connecticut	**Connecticut Office of the Healthcare Advocate** *Mailing Address:* P.O. Box 1543 Hartford, CT 06144 (866) 466-4446 www.ct.gov/oha healthcare.advocate@ct.gov

Appendix | Consumer Assistance Programs and State Departments of Insurance

State	Contact Information
Delaware	**Insurance Commissioner and Department of Insurance** *Main Office* *Street Address:* 841 Silver Lake Blvd. Dover, DE 19904 (302) 674-7300 *Wilmington Office* *Street Address:* Carvel State Office Building, 5th Floor 820 N. French Street Wilmington, DE 19801 (302) 577-5280 (302) 674-7310 (800) 282-8611 consumer@state.de.us www.delawareinsurance.gov
District of Columbia	**DC Office of the Health Care Ombudsman and Bill of Rights** *Street Address:* 899 North Capitol Street, NE, 6th Floor, Room 6037 Washington, DC 20002 (877) 685-6391 healthcareombudsman@dc.gov
Florida	**Florida Office of Insurance Regulation** www.floir.com *Send consumer questions/complaints to:* Florida Department of Financial Services Division of Consumer Services 200 East Gaines Street Tallahassee, FL 32399-4288 (877) MY-FL-CFO (1-877-693-5236) Out of State Callers: (850) 413-3089 TDD: (800) 640-0886 www.myfloridacfo.com/consumers/needourhelp.htm
Georgia	**Georgia Office of Insurance and Safety Fire Commissioner** *Consumer Services Division* *Street Address:* 2 Martin Luther King, Jr. Drive West Tower, Suite 716 Atlanta, GA 30334 (800) 656-2298 www.oci.ga.gov/ConsumerService/Home.aspx

State	Contact Information
Guam	**Guam Department of Insurance** *Street Address:* 1240 Army Drive Barrigada, Guam 96913 *Mailing Address:* Dept. of Revenue & Taxation Taxpayer Services Division P.O. Box 23607 GMF, Guam 96921 Fax: 671-633-2643 pinadm@revtax.gov.gu www.guamtax.com
Hawaii	**Hawaii Department of Commerce and Consumer Affairs** *Mailing Address:* Hawaii Insurance Division Health Insurance Branch P.O. Box 3614 Honolulu, HI 96811 (808) 586-2790 (808) 586-2799 http://hawaii.gov/dcca/ins
Idaho	**Idaho Department of Insurance** *Mailing Address:* P.O. Box 83720 Boise, ID 83720-0043 (800) 721-3272 (208) 334-4250 www.doi.idaho.gov
Illinois	**Illinois Department of Insurance** *Street Address:* 100 Randolph Street, 9th Floor Chicago, IL 60601 (877) 527-9431 www.insurance.illinois.gov
Indiana	**Indiana Department of Insurance** *Street Address:* 311 W. Washington Street, Suite 100 Indianapolis, IN 46204 (800) 622-4461 idoi@idoi.in.gov www.in.gov/idoi

Appendix | Consumer Assistance Programs and State Departments of Insurance

State	Contact Information
Iowa	**Iowa State Insurance Division** Consumer Advocate Bureau Street Address: 330 Maple Street Des Moines, Iowa 50319 (515) 281-5705 (877) 955-1212 http://insuranceca.iowa.gov consumer.advocate@iid.iowa.gov
Kansas	**Kansas Insurance Department** Consumer Assistance Division Street Address: 420 SW 9th Street Topeka, KS 66612 In-state: (800) 432-2484 All others: (785) 296-7829 www.ksinsurance.org CAP@ksinsurance.org
Kentucky	**Kentucky Health Insurance Advocate** Department of Insurance Street Address: 215 West Main Street Frankfort, KY 40601 Mailing address: P.O. Box 517 Frankfort, KY 40602-0517 (877) 587-7222 (800) 648-6056 (TYY) http://healthinsurancehelp.ky.gov DOI.CAPOmbudsman@ky.gov
Louisiana	**Louisiana Department of Insurance** Office of Health Insurance Street Address: 1702 N. Third Street Baton Rouge, LA 70802 Mailing Address: P.O. Box 94214 Baton Rouge, LA 70804 (225) 219-4770 (800) 259-5301 www.ldi.louisiana.gov

State	Contact Information
Maine	**Consumers for Affordable Health Care** Street Address: 12 Church Street Augusta, ME 04338-2490 (800) 965-7476 Mailing Address: P.O. Box 2490 Augusta, ME 04338-2490 www.mainecahc.org consumerhealth@mainecahc.org
Maryland	**Maryland Office of the Attorney General** Health Education and Advocacy Unit Street Address: 200 St. Paul Place, 16th Floor Baltimore, MD 21202 (877) 261-8807 www.oag.state.md.us/Consumer.HEAU.htm heau@oag.state.md.us
Massachusetts	**Massachusetts Consumer Assistance** Street Address: 30 Winter Street, Suite 1004 Boston, MA 02108 (888) 211-6168 www.massconsumerassistance.org
Michigan	**Michigan Health Insurance Consumer Assistance Program (HICAP)** Michigan Office of Financial and Insurance Regulation Mailing Address: P.O. Box 30220 Lansing, MI 48909 (877) 999-6442 http://michigan.gov/ofir Ofir-hicap@michigan.gov

Appendix | Consumer Assistance Programs and State Departments of Insurance

State	Contact Information
Minnesota	**Minnesota Department of Commerce (for fully insured plans)** Street Address: 85 7th Place East, Suite 500 St. Paul, MN 55101 (651) 296-2488 (800) 657-3602 TTY: (651) 296-2860 www.state.mn.us/portal/mn/jsp/home.do?agency=Insurance **Minnesota Department of Health (for state-regulated HMO)** Managed Care Systems Section Mailing Address: P.O. Box 64882 St. Paul, MN 55164-0882 (651) 201-5178 www.health.state.mn.us/index.html
Mississippi	**Health Help Mississippi** Street Address: 800 North President St Jackson, MS 39202 (877) 314-3843 www.healthhelpms.org healthhelpms@mhap.org
Missouri	**Missouri Department of Insurance** Street Address: Harry S. Truman State Office Building 301 W. High Street, Room 830 Jefferson City, MO 65101 (800) 726-7390 www.insurance.mo.gov consumeraffairs@insurance.mo.gov
Montana	**Montana Commissioner of Securities and Insurance** Street Address: 840 Helena Avenue Helena, MT 59601 In-state: (800) 332-6148 (406) 444-2040 TDD: (406) 444-3246 www.csi.mt.gov/consumers/consumers.asp

Healthcare, Insurance, and You | 159

State	Contact Information
Nebraska	**State Department of Insurance** *Nebraska Department of Insurance* *Mailing Address:* P.O. Box 82089 Lincoln, NE 68501-2089 (877) 564-7323 (800) 833-7352 www.doi.ne.gov
Nevada	**Office of Consumer Health Assistance** *Governor's Consumer Health Advocate* *Street Address:* 555 East Washington Ave #4800 Las Vegas, NV 89101 (702) 486-3587 (888) 333-1597 www.govcha.nv.gov cha@govcha.nv.gov
New Hampshire	**New Hampshire State Insurance Department** *Street Address:* 21 South Fruit Street, Suite 14 Concord, NH 03301 (800) 852-3416 TTY/TDD: 1-800-735-2964 www.nh.gov/insurance consumerservices@ins.nh.gov
New Jersey	**New Jersey State Insurance Department** *Office of Consumer Protection Services* *NJ Department of Banking and Insurance* *Mailing Address:* P.O. Box 329 Trenton, NJ 08625-0329 (609) 292-7272 Consumer Hotline: (800) 446-7467 www.state.nj.us/dobi/consumer.htm

Appendix | Consumer Assistance Programs and State Departments of Insurance

State	Contact Information
New Mexico	**NMPRC Insurance Division** *Health Insurance Consumer Assistance Program* *Street Address:* 1120 Paseo De Peralta Santa Fe, NM 87504 (855) 857-0972 (888) 427-5772 Fax: (505) 476-0326 http://nmprc.state.nm.us/id.htm mchb.grievance@state.nm.us
New York	**Community Service Society of New York, Community Health Advocates** *Street Address:* 105 East 22nd Street, 8th floor New York, NY 10010 (888) 614-5400 www.communityhealthadvocates.org cha@cssny.org
North Carolina	**North Carolina Department of Insurance** *Health Insurance Smart NC* *Street Address:* 1201 Mail Service Center Raleigh, NC 27699-1201 (877) 885-0231 http://ncdoi.com/Smart/
North Dakota	**North Dakota Insurance Department** *Street Address:* State Capitol, fifth floor 600 E. Boulevard Ave. Bismarck, ND 58505-0320 (701) 328-2440 (800) 247-0560 TTY: (800) 366-6888 www.nd.gov/ndins insurance@nd.gov

Healthcare, Insurance, and You

State	Contact Information
Ohio	**Ohio Department of Insurance** _Street Address:_ 50 W. Town Street, Third Floor, Suite 300 Columbus, OH 43215 Toll-Free: (800) 686-1526 TDD: (614) 644-3745 www.insurance.ohio.gov/Pages life.health.mcd@insurance.ohio.gov
Oklahoma	**Oklahoma Insurance Department** _Street Address:_ Five Corporate Plaza 3625 Northwest 56th Street, Suite 100 Oklahoma City, OK 73112 In-state: (800) 522-0071 (405) 521-2991 www.ok.gov/oid/Consumers/Consumer_Assistance/index.html
Oregon	**Oregon Health Connect** _Street Address:_ 1435 NE 81st Avenue, Suite 500 Portland, OR 97213-6759 (855) 999-3210 oregonhealthconnect.org healthconnect@211info.org
Pennsylvania	**Pennsylvania Department of Insurance** _Street Address:_ 1209 Strawberry Square Harrisburg, PA 17111 (877) 881-6388 www.insurance.pa.gov
Puerto Rico	**Puerto Rico Department of Insurance** _Office of the Commissioner of Insurance_ _Street Address:_ B5 Calle Tabonuco Suite 216, PMB 356 Guaynabo, PR 00968-3029 (787) 304-8686

Appendix | Consumer Assistance Programs and State Departments of Insurance

State	Contact Information
Rhode Island	**Rhode Island Consumer Assistance Program** *Rhode Island Parent Information Network, Inc.* *Street Address:* 1210 Pontiac Avenue Cranston, RI 02920 (855) 747-3224 www.RIREACH.org
South Carolina	**South Carolina Department of Insurance** *Street Address:* 1201 Main Street, Suite 1000 Columbia, SC 29201 *Mailing Address:* P.O. Box 100105 Columbia, SC 29202 *Consumer Services:* (800) 768-3467 (803) 737-6180 consumers@doi.sc.gov
South Dakota	**South Dakota Division of Insurance** *Street Address:* 445 East Capitol Avenue Pierre, SD 57501 (605) 773-3563 www.state.sd.us/drr2/reg/insurance insurance@state.sd.us
Tennessee	**Tennessee Department of Commerce and Insurance** *Consumer Insurance Services* *Street Address:* 500 James Robertson Parkway, 4th Floor Nashville, Tennessee 37243 (800) 342-4029 (615) 741-2218 Fax: (615) 532-7389
Texas	**Texas Department of Insurance** *Street Address:* 333 Guadalupe Austin, TX 78701 (800) 578-4677 www.tdi.texas.gov/index.html

State	Contact Information
Utah	**Utah Insurance Department** *Street Address:* State Office Building, Room 3110 Salt Lake City, UT 84114 Health Insurance Division Consumer Service: (801) 538-3077 TDD: (801) 538-3826 www.insurance.utah.gov health.uid@utah.gov
Vermont	Vermont Legal Aid *Street Address:* 264 North Winooski Ave. Burlington, VT 05402 (800) 917-7787 www.vtlegalaid.org
Virginia	**Virginia State Corporation Commission** *Bureau of Insurance* *Street Address:* Tyler Building, 1300 East Main Street Richmond, Virginia 23219 (800) 552-7945 (Virginia only) (804) 371-9741 www.scc.virginia.gov/boi/index.aspx Bureauofinsurance@scc.virginia.gov
Virgin Islands	**U.S. Virgin Islands Division of Banking and Insurance** *Street Address:* 1131 King Street, Suite 101 Christiansted St. Croix, VI 00820 (340) 773-6459 http://ltg.gov.vi
Washington	**Washington State Office of the Insurance Commissioner** *Street Address:* 5000 Capitol Blvd., SE Tumwater, WA 98501 1-800-562-6900 360-725-7080 TDD: 360-586-0241 www.insurance.wa.gov/consumers/CAP-contact-us.shtml cap@oic.wa.gov

Appendix | Consumer Assistance Programs and State Departments of Insurance

State	Contact Information
West Virginia	**West Virginia Department of Insurance** *Mailing Address:* P.O. Box 50540 Charleston, WV 25305-0540 *Street Address:* 1124 Smith Street Charleston, WV 25301 (304) 558-3386 (888) TRY-WVIC (1-888-879-9842) TDD: (304) 558-1296 TDD: (800) 435-7381
Wisconsin	**Wisconsin Office of the Commissioner of Insurance** *Street Address:* 125 South Webster Street Madison, WI 53703 (800) 236-8517 TDD: Dial 711 and ask for (608) 266-3586 http://oci.wi.gov/consinfo.htm ocicomplaints@wisconsin.gov
Wyoming	**Wyoming Insurance Department** *Street Address:* 106 East 6th Avenue Cheyenne, WY 82002 (307) 777-7401 In-state: (800) 438-5768 http://insurance.state.wy.us wyinsdep@state.wy.us

I

Index

A

Adjusted gross income (AGI), 39
Advance care directives, 138
Advance directives
   advance care directives, 138
   definition, 136
   financial, 137
   online resources, 139
   types, 137
Affordable Care Act (ACA). *See also* Work-based health insurance
   chronic health condition, 18
   fairer pricing, 20
   features, 20
   health insurance marketplaces
      application process, 28
      benefits, 25, 28
      cost, 26
      open enrollment, 25
      out-of-pocket expense, 28
   health plan, 30
   individual mandate, 35
   infograph, 33
   insurance coverage, 19
   Kaiser Family Foundation
      analysis, 30
      Certified Application Counselor, 29
      consumer assistance program, 29
      navigator and in-person assister, 29
   Medicaid
      definition, 21
      eligibility, 21
      enrollment process, 24
      factors, 22
      poverty level, 22
      qualification, 24
      state participation, 22
   Medicare program, 18
   penalty schedule, 23, 32
   primary parts, 18

B

Billing errors
   ask for a discount, 107
   balance billing, 109
   big chunk, 102
   claims processing, 102
   CPT codes, 106
   denied insurance claims
      complaint, 113
      covered benefit, 112
      external appeal, 114
      GAO, 111
      internal appeal, 113
      network provider, 112
      step therapy, 112
   EOBs, 105
   experts, 114
   healthcare prices, 107
   hospital stays, 103
   in-network rate, 106
   itemized bill, 104
   medical records, 115
   paying close attention, 102
   prices, 101

Index

Billing errors (cont.)
   resolving billing disputes
      chief financial
         officer, 110
      doctor for help, 110
      documentation, 110
      file complaint, 111
      holding, 111
      insurance company, 110
      negotiation, 111
      rights, 111
   review statement, 103
Bronze-level plan, 69

C

Certified Application Counselor (CACs), 29
Common Procedural Terminology (CPT) code, 86, 105, 107
Commonwealth Fund, 2
Consumer Assistance Programs (CAPs), 114
Current Procedural Terminology (CPT), 86

D

Drug prescription
   consumer reports, 90
   co-pays, 92
   medication
      big-box giant Costco, 93
      cost saving, 91, 97
      discount drug card, 95
      doctor and pharmacist, 91
      donut hole, 94
      formulary, 91
      GoodRX, 95
      LowestMed, 96
      Medicare Extra Help, 94
      out-of-pocket, 92
      pill splitting, 97–98
      Prescription Saver, 96
      prices, 93
      VIPPS seal, 96
   non-adherence, 90
   websites, 98

E

Employees benefits
   affordable insurance, 58
   annual limits, 56
   appealing insurance denials, 57
   children younger than 19, 57
   deductibles, 60
   freedom and protection, 60
   lifetime limits, 56
   limited insurance cost, 59
   money toward care, 60
   out-of-pocket medical costs, 59
   preventive care, 56
   tax-preferred health accounts, 60
   waiting periods, 58
   young adults, 57
Employers
   ACA's impact, 53
   insurance cost
      large employers, 63
      mid-sized employers, 65
      small employers, 65
   not offering penalties, 54
Explanation of Benefits (EOB), 105–106

F

Family coverage
   married, no children, 46
   married, one child, 46
   married, two children, 45
   single, two children, 44
Financial advance directives, 137
Flexible Spending Arrangement (FSA), 60
Future planning
   advance directives
      advance care directives, 138
      definition, 136
      financial, 137
      online resources, 139
      types, 137
   Alzheimer's-related dementia, United States, 139
   choosing nursing home
      options, 145
      quality, 146
      staff turnover, 147

Index

cost of Alzheimer's
    cost of caring, 139
    doctor's visits and outpatient
      medical services, 140
    drug plans, 141
    in home services, 140
    long-term nursing home care, 140
    online resources, 141
getting affairs, 135
hospice care
    definition, 148
    delivery places, 148
    healthcare professionals team, 148
    online resources, 149
long-term care insurance
    (see Long-term care insurance)

G

Gold-level plan, 69
GoodRX, 95
Government Accountability Office (GAO), 111

H

Healthcare system
    capacity, 1
    reform (see Health reform)
    rising costs, 14
Health Maintenance Organization (HMO), 119
Health plans
    grandfathered health plans, 61
    rating rules, 61
    self-insured health plan, 61
    types, 61
Health reform
    Affordable Care Act, 12
    aspects of, 3
    buy health insurance, 13
    changes
      disqualify plan, 9
      drug cost relief, 10
      grandfathered plans, 7
      insurance company, 5
      lifetime limit, 6
      parents' health plan, 10
      preventive care, 6
      private insurance market, 4
      right to appeal, 10
    costs, 3
    insuring the uninsured, 4
    medical condition, 12
    paid delivery, 12
Health Savings Accounts (HSAs), 28
Hospice care
    definition, 148
    delivery places, 148
    healthcare professionals team, 148
    online resources, 149
Hybrid plans, 144

I

Institute of Medicine (IOM), 2
Internal Revenue Service, 53

J

Jargon alert
    co-pay, 6
    creditable coverage, 124
    Current Procedural Terminology, 86
    EOB, 105
    formulary, 92
    grandfathered health plans, 7
    health insurance marketplaces, 13, 20
    Medicaid, 21
    Medicare, 119
    premium, 2, 35
    private insurance market, 19
    provider network, 128
    self-insured health plans, 61

K

Kaiser Family Foundation, 29

L

Longevity insurance, 144
Long-term care insurance
    agents and information, 144
    benefits, 142
    cost of care considerations
      age, 143
      employer, 143
      existing costs, 143
      professional help, 144
      rising costs, 143

Index

Long-term care insurance (cont.)
   inflation-adjusted policy, 142
   Kiplinger's report, 142
   Medicaid qualification, 142
   waiting period, 142
LowestMed, 96

M, N, O

Medicaid. See Affordable Care Act (ACA)
Medical costs
   benefits, 76
   co-insurance, 76
   co-pays, 76
   deductibles, 76
   healthcare prices, 77
   insurance plan
      advocates, 84
      billing error, 83
      expensive location, 86
      healthcare price, 84
      health plan's rules, 79
      in-network doctor, 81
      lower price, 86
      out-of-network care, 82
      recommended treatment, 80
   insurance premiums, 75
   treatment, 77
Medicare
   drug coverage plan, 130
   eHealth, 122
   employer-based insurance, 129
   employer-sponsor insurance, 130
   enrollment periods
      benefits, 127
      cost, 128
      disenrollment, 125
      open enrollment, 125
      option coverage, 126
      prescription medications, 128
      retirement, 128
      star ratings, 126
   health insurance program, 117
   insurance card, 122
   Medigap, 121
   MSP program, 131
   observation services, 132
   parts of
      Advantage plans, 119
      hospital care services, 118
      monthly premium, 118
      prescription drug costs, 120
   penalty
      creditable coverage, 124
      Medigap plan, 124
      paying, 123
   personal assistance, 130
   PlanPrescriber, 132
   time limits, 130
   work-based coverage, 129
Medicare Savings Programs (MSPs), 128, 131
Modified gross income (MAGI), 39

P, Q

Platinum-level plan, 69
Preferred Provider Organization (PPO), 119
Prescription Saver, 96

R

Resource alert, 122–123

S

Shared benefit plans, 144
Shared responsibility, 53
Silver-level plan, 69
Skilled nursing facility (SNF), 133
Small Business Health Options Program (SHOP) exchanges
   companies with fewer than 50 employees, 67
   employee choice, 68
   everyone is approved, 68
   fluctuating hours, 71
   licensed insurance broker, 69
   70% participation, 69
   standardized plans, 67
   tallying employees' time, 69
State Health Insurance Counseling and Assistance Programs (SHIPS), 130
Step therapy, 92

T

Tax credits
  advantage, 48
  impacts of taking, 49
  income
    AGI, 39
    family coverage (see Family coverage)
    health plans, 41
    individual coverage, 43
    MAGI, 39
    out-of-pocket spending limits, 42–43
    poverty level, 42
    qualification, 39
    silver-level insurance plan, 39, 41
    state's marketplace, 43
  metal level plans, 42
  paying, 37
  report changes, 50
  requirements, 47
  resources, 50
  salary increment, 49

U

Usual, customary, and reasonable (UCR) charges, 82

V

Verified Internet Pharmacy Practices Site (VIPPS), 96

W, X, Y, Z

Work-based health insurance
  costs
    large employers, 63
    mid-sized employers, 65
    small employers, 65

employees benefits
  affordable insurance, 58
  annual limits, 56
  appealing insurance denials, 57
  children younger than 19, 57
  deductibles, 60
  freedom and protection, 60
  lifetime limits, 56
  limited insurance cost, 59
  money toward care, 60
  out-of-pocket medical costs, 59
  preventive care, 56
  tax-preferred health accounts, 60
  waiting periods, 58
  young adults, 57
employers
  ACA's impact, 53
  not offering penalties, 54
health plans and employers
  (see Health plans)
role of business, 51
small business
  administrative expenses, 66
  50 or fewer full-time employees, 66
  optional offering, 73
  SHOP exchanges (see Small Business Health Options Program (SHOP) exchanges)
  tax credits, 72

Other Apress Business Titles You Will Find Useful

Health Care Reform Simplified, 2nd Edition
Parks
978-1-4302-4896-5

Control Your Retirement Destiny
Anspach
978-1-4302-5022-7

Common Sense
Tanner
978-1-4302-4152-2

Power Plays
Rapier
978-1-4302-4086-0

Broken Markets
Mellyn
978-1-4302-4221-5

Underwater
Lauer
978-1-4302-4470-7

Fixing and Flipping Real Estate
Boardman
978-1-4302-4644-2

Plan Your Own Estate
Wheatley-Liss
978-1-4302-4494-3

Tax Insight
Murdock
978-1-4302-6310-4

Available at www.apress.com

GPSR Compliance
The European Union's (EU) General Product Safety Regulation (GPSR) is a set of rules that requires consumer products to be safe and our obligations to ensure this.

If you have any concerns about our products, you can contact us on

ProductSafety@springernature.com

In case Publisher is established outside the EU, the EU authorized representative is:

Springer Nature Customer Service Center GmbH
Europaplatz 3
69115 Heidelberg, Germany

www.ingramcontent.com/pod-product-compliance
Lightning Source LLC
LaVergne TN
LVHW040738250326
834688LV00031B/360